Exploring La
A Comple

CU00556789

Exploring LAKELAND TARNS

A Complete Guide

Don Blair

Ellenbank
Press

For Meg

Published by Ellenbank Press
The Lathes, Selby Terrace, Maryport
Cumbria CA15 6LX

First published 1993

Maps by Ian Rankin
Designed by Sheila Sherwen

Typeset in 10/11½pt Garamond by
Deltatype Ltd, Ellesmere Port, Cheshire
Printed and bound in Great Britain by
Athenaeum Press Ltd, Newcastle upon Tyne

British Library Cataloguing in Publication Data
A catalogue record for this book is available
from the British Library.

ISBN 1 873551 05 3

Contents

Acknowledgements

First and foremost, I thank my wife Gladys for taking on the onerous task of typing the manuscript and especially for her sympathetic handling of fraught situations. I acknowledge the guidance given by the dedicated staff and librarian of the Freshwater Biological Association when the way ahead was unclear. To those who offered practical help and encouragement: the Principal of the Brathay Hall Field Study Centre for details of Mortimere; the National Maritime Museum for notes on the Kentmere Boat and Les Ridding, the discoverer, for details of its excavation; and to various farmers for their 'crack' and snippets of intelligence on tarns and related subjects, my thanks. I tender my sincere appreciation to Steve Douglas of the National Rivers Authority, and all the secretaries of local angling associations and owners of tackle shops, who showed such forbearance while being badgered for information by a non-angler. Finally, a special thank you to Walter White for his knowledgeable advice, and Warren Elsby for reading the manuscript.

Note: The details of routes given in this guide do not imply a right of way. Readers are reminded to seek permission where necessary to use footpaths.

Every effort has been made to ensure that the information presented in this book is accurate and up to date. However, if you find any changes that you feel should be included in the next edition, the publishers will be pleased to hear from you.

Readers are reminded that the publishers cannot take responsibility for accident or injury sustained on any of the walks. Care should always be taken to check weather conditions before setting out on the walks, especially in remote or hilly areas.

Please note that the sketch maps for the Tarn Walks are for general guidance only. The walks should not be attempted without the appropriate Ordnance Survey map.

Introduction

One damp, misty November afternoon I met a fellow walker on Greenup Edge. He appeared out of the gloom some 30 paces ahead, carrying a laden rucksack easily. We stopped and spoke – of boots and routes and objectives, glad of a few moments' companionship to relieve the loneliness. He, young, vigorous and intelligent; myself, grey, too old to be out alone in such a place on such a day.

'Have you visited Dock Tarn – over there?' he asked, waving his hand in the general direction. I replied that I had not. 'Worth a visit,' he suggested. Then we parted, he with a warning to 'watch the cliffs on Standing Crag'.

The conversation encouraged me; some months later I visited Dock Tarn, at this time frozen with a snow dusting on the ice and broken sedge protruding like inverted Vs. The sun-sparkling scene captivated me; how I wished I had a camera to record the silent beauty of that place, held fast in the February frost. Here the seed sown on Greenup Edge began to germinate and the remainder of that winter was given over to 'collecting' tarns.

I had long since 'done' my Wainwrights; the convenience and privilege of living and working in the region had made this achievable. Although the joy of this land was not dulled by familiarity, I now found a new enthusiasm and delight in tramping fells that I had known for years.

The fascination of tarns lies in their diversity of size and setting, their changing moods occasioned by weather and season, and in the variety of plant and animal life they sustain. Some may be visited with little effort while others require the route-finding expertise of the practised hill-walker. The mild excitement of the hunt provides a special satisfaction.

To those lovers of Lakeland who seek new horizons, who wish to explore its less frequented byways, I commend the tarns.

There are a number of people whose works have influenced my observations in this guide or who deserve a place for one reason or

7

another in the annals of 'tarnology'. I mention them in chronological order, as far as possible.

First was the late Professor J. E. Marr who pioneered the geomorphological study of tarns in Lakeland and published papers on them in 1895 and 1896 (see Bibliography). Earlier works had suggested that tarns resulting from the last glacial period were formed from ice-scooped rock basins. For the tarns he studied, Marr disproved this theory. Instead he showed how former valleys had become blocked or dammed by moraine material, resulting in the formation of lakes or tarns behind the blockages. It so happens that the lowest point of escape for the impounded water is sometimes across the rock of the fellside, to one side of the infilled former valley, giving the impression of a rock basin. This point he demonstrated very clearly for a number of tarns, such as Devoke Water, Small Water and Codale Tarn. There are several tarns he did not examine, however, and it is just possible that there may be a true rock basin among them.

The classic guide to Lakeland tarns, *The Tarns of Lakeland* (published in 1960), was written and illustrated by the Grasmere author and artist Mr W. Heaton Cooper. Apart from visiting all these delightful waters myself, I have drawn heavily on this book for background information. The illustrations are masterly; it has been part of the enjoyment for me to try to replicate these with a camera and see how the scene has evolved through time.

In Heaton Cooper's introduction he mentions 'two hardy men of Grasmere' who used to spend their weekends seeking out tarns in which to bathe.The story of Timothy Tyson, village shoemaker, and Colin Dodgson who kept a tea garden in Grasmere, is told in A. H. Griffin's *Inside the Real Lakeland*. Once wartime petrol rationing was eased in 1951, these two men began to seek out every lake, tarn or pond they could find. In eight years they took a total of 463 plunges. I was fortunate enough to locate Colin Dodgson, survivor of this epic enterprise, who told me that they continued the project until 1966, by which time they had achieved a grand total of 730 plunges. Timothy died in 1967, a year after the project was completed, at the age of 83. Colin, who was 23 years his junior, can claim many other mountain achievements, for he completed all the Scottish Munros, the English 2,000 footers and the Welsh and Irish 2,500 footers before he died at the age of 81.

Finally, mention must be made of Ralph Stokoe, a keen amateur naturalist who lived in Cockermouth. In 1975 he began a five-year study of the plants contained in nearly 300 Cumbrian lakes, tarns and reservoirs, visiting many of them several times. His record of visits ceased in 1980 with his untimely death; however the results of his work have been collated from his meticulous record cards and published in a booklet by the Freshwater Biological Association at Far Sawrey, Ambleside. This is probably the most complete list of Cumbrian water bodies and their flora in existence.

WHAT IS A TARN?

It's surprising how frequently this question crops up. 'A small mountain lake' says the dictionary, which is more or less what one would imagine a tarn to be. However, in practice, the term seems to be applied to standing waters, as opposed to flowing waters, which range in size from what a person might fairly judge to be a lake to that of a large puddle. More discriminating questioners look for certain features to provide conclusive evidence that a particular standing water is a tarn and not a lake, or a mere, or any other kind of water you care to mention. Perhaps it is as unproductive as asking when a rill becomes a stream – becomes a river, or a hillock becomes a hill – becomes a mountain. In these cases, it is simply a matter of magnitude.

When discussing standing waters, there are also regional, historical and cultural factors to be considered. 'Tarn' is a regional term peculiar to the Lake District although not exclusively so, for examples may be traced eastwards into the Pennines and thence southwards as far as Keighley in Yorkshire, where there is an example known as Redcar or Keighley Tarn. Other terms have evolved from different cultures: lochs and lochans are native to the Scots, loughs to the Irish Celts, llyns to the Welsh, while, meres are Early English and more common in the English lowlands. 'Tarn' is derived from the Old Norse *tjorn*. Along with many other Lake District placenames, it originated with the Viking – or Norse – invaders who made their home in Cumbria in the early part of the tenth century AD.

All we can safely say is that the names given to most Lakeland waters seem to have been decided on centuries ago somewhat arbitrarily (for some tarns are larger than some lakes), to be passed on from generation to generation, embedded in the literature and engraved on the maps.

Perhaps the best distinction between a tarn and a lake was that suggested by T. T. Macan of the Freshwater Biological Association, who pointed out that the most common emergent plant in tarns tended to be the bottle sedge, *Carex rostrata*, whereas in lakes it is often the common reed, *Phragmites australis*. However, many tarns and lakes contain both. A related factor is that of altitude. Upland waters, scarce in plant nutrients, do not favour the reed, yet the sedge will thrive; sedge will also live happily in some lowland waters where the reed grows best. Surface area and degree of permanence could also be considered as factors in the definition of a tarn.

Before man found a use for stored water all tarns were, in effect, natural ponds; how different is the situation today. I would estimate that over 40 per cent of tarns have been altered in some way by human activity, either by raising the original embankment in order to increase storage capacity for sporting or industrial purposes, or by deepening or straightening the outflow to drain ponds and make more land available for agriculture. Many so-called tarns are purely artificial anyway. For example, Yew Tree Tarn near Coniston was created as a fish pond by the raising of a stone-faced concrete dam in the 1930s. More recently, in 1987–8, a conservation-minded farmer built Atkinson Tarn near Crook.

Yet the term 'tarn' persists, and there seems little to be gained in attempting to give it a precise scientific definition. Perhaps we should simply accept the view of Heaton Cooper the artist: that it is the emotional response which finally defines it, as anything that has the feel and character of a tarn and gives delight.

HOW TARNS CAME TO BE

The present-day surface features of Cumbria – the shape of its fells and dales, its lakes and tarns, rivers and becks – date from the end of the last ice age. When the glaciers and ice sheets finally receded some 10,000 years ago, they left a sculpted landscape littered with debris and practically bereft of soil and vegetation.

Highland areas were particularly affected because they attracted high snowfall which became compacted into ice. In the Lakeland region the ice moved downwards and outwards from areas of high accumulation, removing all loose material in the process. Glaciers, which had been formed within the confines of former valleys, scoured, shattered and smoothed the bare bones of the mountains until, after some 8,000 years, the freezing climate began to ease its grip. Summers grew warmer and winters less severe.

Deprived of snowfall, the lowland ice sheets thinned and faded, leaving their burden of debris spread in hummocky mounds. As they melted, the valley glaciers retreated slowly to their highland fastness where temperatures were still low enough for them to persist for another thousand years or so, scouring and scraping, removing and transporting rock, often depositing it in barrier-like mounds called moraines, at their melting point, or snout. The result was hundreds of water-retaining depressions, often larger on lower ground and in valleys where greater masses of ice scoured more deeply and deposited more rock debris.

These processes were not, of course, unique to the region. Other areas subjected to glaciation display similar features, such as U-shaped valleys and long, narrow finger lakes. The only truly unique feature of the Lake District is the radial pattern of its lakes, caused by its former dome-like structure and consequent drainage pattern. The tarns are certainly not unique – except in name – existing elsewhere in Britain as lochans, llyns or loughs.

Many tarns share certain similarities which could suggest common origins, and one can attempt an elementary classification of tarn types based mainly on their particular location in an upland area and as a direct result of glaciation. An obvious example is the corrie (cirque or combe) tarn found in an armchair-shaped hollow, such as Blea Water and Langdale's Angle and Stickle Tarns. Another type, less distinctive than the corrie tarn, is to be found on the shelves above glacial valleys, such as Alcock and Lingmoor Tarns. Then there are those that occupy depressions on whaleback ridges between valleys, such as Burnmoor Tarn, Angle Tarn (Patterdale) and Beacon Tarn. Some are to be found on cols (low points on a ridge, often termed a hawse or hause in Cumbria): Beckhead and Kirkfell Tarns and the diminutive Carlside Tarn on Skiddaw are examples of this type. A feature of col tarns – always small due to their confined situation – is their tendency to elongate at right angles to the ridge on which they rest. This is due to the prevailing wind whipping over the col and setting up a wave action which erodes the lee shore.

Of clearly post-glacial origin are those tarns which occupy depressions within organic material, such as peat bog, where small areas of the peat surface have deteriorated and the resulting hollows become water-filled to the level of the local water table. These tarns, limited by the depth of the peat, are shallow and seldom exceed 1m (3ft) in Lakeland. Examples of such peat bog tarns are Launchy and High Scawdel Tarns above Borrowdale and Red Crag Tarn on High Street.

On the lowland areas at the fringes of the fells, where sand, gravel or clay has been dumped by melting glaciers or ice sheets, many beautiful and varied tarns are to be found. These lowland sites, richer in mineral nutrients and exposed to less extreme weather conditions than their upland cousins, support a more luxuriant range of marginal and aquatic vegetation. Often situated in hummocky terrain, surrounded by trees, edged by reeds and bright with water lilies, they present a softness of character in sharp contrast to the stark, stone-edged beauty of the high tarns.

Finally, there is a considerable variation in the number of tarns located in each of the three main geological regions of Lakeland although each region occupies a broadly similar surface area. Only about 10 per cent of tarns are situated in the Skiddaw Slates; about 40 per cent occur on the Silurian rocks of Southern Lakeland, though most of these may be described as lowland tarns. It is within the Borrowdale Volcanic Group that the largest proportion (about 50 per cent) occur, and most of these could be loosely classified as high tarns. Future research may provide some explanation of the reasons for this uneven distribution.

There is one important respect in which geology influences tarns and that is in their water chemistry. In simple terms, the rocks on which a tarn lies, or from which it receives its water, determine whether that tarn's water is soft and acid or perhaps hard or alkaline with a lime content. This factor, coupled with the climatic influence of altitude, affects the vegetation, which is such a prominent visual feature of these fascinating waters and is so often a point of contrast between highland and lowland tarns.

The Tarn-Dwellers

One cannot talk of tarns without mentioning the plants that live within and around them, for they would be dull indeed if their sometimes harsh outlines were not softened by the varied textures and colours of their vegetation.

A distinctive feature of some lowland tarns is the 'wetland' or 'carr' which develops around them. These tarns lie in shallow basins surrounded by agricultural pasture land. In this situation steady plant growth, perhaps accelerated in recent times by fertilisers and other nutrients washed down into the tarn, produces a border of dense reeds backed by woodland consisting mainly of willow, alder and birch. This type of wetland or carr develops on a peaty base formed from the partly decayed remains of encroaching reeds and other water plants. Good examples of this type of tarn are Skelsmergh, Peggy and Grayrigg Tarns in the east and, in particular, Priest Pot and Out Dubs Tarn in the Esthwaite Water basin.

Of course trees and reeds are by no means the only forms of plant life associated with tarns. Over the years I have become increasingly aware of the extraordinary variety of plants found in and around their waters. At first, having no botanical knowledge, I simply accepted them as part of the universal greenery. However, as I visited more and more tarns, I gradually realised that the plants of the waterside were quite distinct from those of the land. The horizontals of the floating lily pads contrast with the verticals of the sedge, the horsetails and the spiky rushes. The flowers, too, have a character quite different from those of the land – exotic, sometimes waxy and almost orchid-like. The beautiful bogbean with its pinky-white flowers blooms in virtual obscurity on the marshy tarn margin. Beside the rocky shore of many a remote upland tarn the water lobelia thrusts its delicate lilac trumpets above the surface, while at the edges of lowland tarns the jaunty flag iris waves its yellow pennants. But surpassing all the other blooms in size, brilliance and beauty is the white water lily with its exquisite cupped petals and bright yellow stamens.

13

This section is by no means intended as a detailed guide to aquatic flora, but a basic knowledge of the most common plants enables one to experience more fully the pleasures of the waterside. The ability to survey an unfamiliar tarn and name the prominent growing plants does wonders for one's self-esteem, not to mention the admiration it may elicit from one's companion!

In order to keep things simple I have restricted the descriptions to one common species in each plant family and of course to those specimens which can be seen without the aid of a hand lens or microscope. For further details of these plants, readers may find it helpful to consult the books by R. and A. Fitter, W. Keble Martin and Geoffrey Fryer listed in the Bibliography.

I have divided the plants into four groups according to their growth habits: marginal, emergent, floating-leaved and submerged.

MARGINAL PLANTS

Growing at the margins of tarns, these plants are partly covered or exposed according to the seasonal rise and fall of the water level.

1   Soft rush *Juncus effusus*
This is the most common of a dozen varieties found in boggy conditions. The tall, dark-green tufts of smooth or faintly ridged, leafless stems bear brownish flowers which erupt sideways some distance below the tip.

2   Yellow flag iris *Iris pseudocorus*
The brash yellow flowers with their accompanying sword-shaped leaves are quite unmistakable. The flowers appear from June to August, mainly beside lowland tarns where the water is rich in nutrients.

3   Water mint *Mentha aquatica*
This looks and smells very like its relation, the garden mint. There are several species of various heights and leaf form, but all send out similar aromatic signals. Water mint occurs along the shoreline and at the marshy margins of lowland tarns. Between July and October it bears tight, rounded bunches of reddish-purple florets.

4   Cotton grass *Eriophorum angustifolium*
Usually found on pond margins or in boggy, peaty, acid areas,
cotton grass is more easily identified in spring when the flowering
stem carries bright yellow anthers, or in summer when the fruiting
head carries tufts of white cottony hairs.

5   Common reed *Phragmites australis*
Extensive beds of these tall grass-like stems are common in
lowland tarns. Their height, up to 3.5m (11–12ft), and feathery
flowerheads produced from August to October, make them easy
to spot. Their broad strap-like leaves die down in winter, but the
stems persist as hard canes. Their root system lies on the water
surface, forming a dense mat which tends to entrap sediment and
extend outwards from the shore to form reed fen (see Priest Pot).

EMERGENT PLANTS

These plants root on the pond bed but thrust their flowering heads
and main bodies above the water surface.

6   Bogbean *Menyanthes trifoliata*
Bogbean can be easily identified by its prominent trifoliate leaves
held erect like green, three-fingered hands. It forms dense beds,
and its leaves and flower spikes protrude above the water surface.
The thick, fleshy rhizomes spread horizontally through the peat
or silt in the shallows, avoiding rocky or gravelly beds. Appearing
from May to June, the divided petals of the bell-like flowers,
grouped at the heads of individual spikes, are covered with thick,
white hairs. Bogbean is widely distributed at altitudes up to about
600m (1,800ft).

7   Common club rush *Scirpus lacustris*
Although similar to the common reed in appearance and height,
these tall green stems are rounded and leafless, and grow up to 3m
(10ft) from the pond bed. The flowers, which seem disappointingly small for such a robust stem, consist of clusters of
small cone-like brown spikelets each attached individually to fine
stalks which splay outwards from the head of the stem. They
flower from late June to August and are found in lowland tarns.

8 Water horsetail *Equisetum fluviatile*
In many respects this plant is similar to its land-based cousin, a
smaller version of the former coal-measure forests. The green,
segmented stems grow up to 1.5m (5ft) tall and are sometimes
mistaken for reeds, but close examination reveals the whorls of
stubby branches radiating outwards from the joints. Some stems
have brown, spore-bearing cones at their tips. When full grown,
they project some 60cm (2ft) above the surface of the water.

9 Bottle sedge *Carex rostrata*
Individual sedges are difficult to identify, not least because there
are some 27 different species found in the region, although the
bottle sedge is probably the most common. The best time to see
and identify this graceful, grey green, grasslike perennial is late
spring and early summer when the male and female catkin-like
flowers, held vertically on a thin triangular stem, are in bloom.
The slim, brown catkins at the top of the stem are male; the
plump, green, bristly 'bottle brushes' lower down are female. This
sedge is often found at the shallow end of a tarn.

10 Common spike rush *Eleocharis pulustris*
This rush grows in groups or small tufts in shallow water or
marsh. The green, round, leafless stems rise to a height of 60cm
(2ft) and protrude above the water surface. During the months of
May to August they are tipped with a dark brown flower or
spikelet.

FLOATING-LEAVED PLANTS

These plants have leaves which float horizontally on the water
surface.

11 Broadleaved or Floating pondweed *Potamogetan natans*
A mass of brownish-green oval floating leaves, each about the size
of an oak leaf, makes this aquatic resemble an autumnal fall from
nearby trees. The stubby flower spikes, the size and shape of a
little finger, are thrust vertically above the water surface in June.

12 Floating bur-reed *Sparganium angustifolium*
Green, strap-like floating leaves signal the presence of this reed

but its round, spiked burrs held above the water in summer make it most easily recognisable.

13   White water lily *Nymphaea alba*
Like the flag iris, these lilies are quite distinctive, with their broad, pad-like leaves and large, white flowers. They occur most frequently on lowland tarns; on the richer waters the flowers attain the size of saucers. Interestingly, there is a small bed of water lilies on Dock Tarn, at an altitude of 403m (1,322ft), which must be the highest in the Lake District.

14   Yellow water lily *Nuphar lutea*
The stubby yellow flowers of this lily have only five or six petals and are much smaller in size than the flamboyant white variety. Their floating leaves are similar in size and shape to the white, and it is sometimes hard to differentiate between them until they flower in June to August.

SUBMERGED PLANTS

In these plants the main body remains wholly submerged.

15   Water lobelia *Lobelia dortmana*
The body of the plant consists of submerged, strap-shaped leaves forming a rosette about the diameter of a jam pot lid. From the centre of each rosette a slender flower spike extends and rises above the surface. Pale lilac tubular-shaped flowers appear from July to August, and this plant is usually found on gravelly beds in the higher tarns.

16   Water milfoil *Myriophyllum alterniflorum*
Water milfoil is often anchored to a mud bottom, from which the main stem, with branches, grows up towards the surface. The leaves are pinnate (arranged on opposite sides of a common stalk), with up to 18 segments. These leaves occur in whorls of four about the main stem, giving the plant a feathery appearance.

17   Quillwort *Isoetes lacustris*
Individual tufts of stiff, green, quill-like leaves, rounded in section, identify this submerged plant, although it may resemble

the rosettes of water lobelia and shoreweed when viewed below the surface.

18   Shoreweed *Littorella uniflora*
This differs from quillwort in that the leaves are more semi-circular in section and in its tendency to spread by means of runners to form a grass-like sward. Unlike the quillwort, which is non-flowering, it will flower when exposed by drought. The single greenish-white blooms appear between June and September; the males stalked, with prominent stamens, the females unstalked.

19   Mud water starwort *Callitriche stagnalis*
One of several varieties of this group of plants usually found growing from a mud bottom. The stem rises vertically, with paired oval leaves at regular intervals. At the tip, which touches the water surface, the leaves form a rosette. The various types differ considerably in appearance, from the tall pale-green variety found in Hard Tarn to the short, bunched, narrow-leaved variety present in Brown Cove Tarn.

INSECT AND FISH LIFE

Common, even on the higher tarns, is the whirligig beetle. Smaller than a shirt button, and lively as a cricket, it darts across the water surface of sheltered inlets like a bright jewel. These delightful insects get their name from the way in which they tend to whirl about one another in electron frenzy. They are best seen on tiny high tarns and provide a fascinating diversion for the passing walker with time to spare. Watch out, too, for the water boatman which propels itself energetically below the surface of the water by means of its inbuilt 'oars'. Both these beetles can fly and are thus able to migrate between tarns.

As for fish, the wild brown trout is a surprising denizen of the deep high tarns. To me it is a wonder that fish can survive in such apparently barren waters. One cold clear November day I stood beside Bleaberry Tarn, Buttermere, and watched the expanding rings of rising trout merge and fade. There I remembered an angler

I had once met who claimed to have fished every tarn in Lakeland. 'In Bleaberry Tarn,' he said, 'the trout are very small and thin with hardly any flesh on them – but good sport.' William Wordsworth, himself an angler, is said to have fished in Red Tarn below Helvellyn.

Inhospitable though these high tarns may appear, they provide an ideal environment for brown trout; the cold conditions and high oxygen content, beaten in by stormy waves and driven rain, provide the optimum conditions for the fish – the only requisite lacking is an adequate food supply.

One may pause to wonder how trout came to be in such inaccessible situations. Perhaps they migrated upstream along a tarn's outflow? Or could fish eggs have been carried there on the feet of birds? In tiny Blind Tarn, at an altitude of 572m (1,876ft), there is neither inflow nor outflow, yet I have seen 20cm (8in) trout rise and swim in this airy water, which is also said to contain char. This rare fish is found only in nearby Coniston, Windermere and Goat's Water below Blind Tarn. Anglers, they say, have a weakness for transferring fish from one water to another!

How to Use This Guide

COVERAGE

Some authorities mention the existence of over 1,000 water bodies – including lakes – in Cumbria. I have restricted this book to tarns within the Lake District National Park, with one or two exceptions which I found interesting. Included are all the tarns which appear on the Ordnance Survey maps used, and those which have acquired names either in 'the literature' or by word of mouth, or have been given a name by the Freshwater Biological Association and recorded on their Tarn Database.

Some reservoirs have also been included; others ignored. Here it is difficult to draw the line, for some named tarns, such as Holme Ground, are in fact disused reservoirs, originally constructed for domestic or industrial purposes. Conversely, some reservoirs in active use are actually enlarged former tarns, and still retain their original names. Examples are Fisher Tarn near Kendal (not included), Seathwaite Tarn, Stickle Tarn (Lang.) and Levers Water.

TRANSPORT

Alfred Wainwright apparently relied entirely on public transport when producing his original guides to the Lake District. Unfortunately this would not be possible today. Limited services still exist in Borrowdale and along the A66 and A591, but public transport can no longer cope with the needs of the walker who wishes to penetrate remoter regions.

Cars must be used but the problem is working out how to use them most effectively. Circular walks, arriving back at the starting point without involving a long road walk, are not always easy to plan. 'There and back' walks can be enjoyable, but leave one feeling that the effort could have been better spent. Sometimes an elected driver is willing to drop walkers in one valley and collect them later from another. It is really up to the individual to find the best solution.

Parking space is usually limited; the early bird – or the person who comes outside high season – gets the space. Unfortunately some motorists tend to leave just less than a car's width between their vehicle and the next. To these thoughtless people, may your batteries flatten and your tyres deflate!

The car has also brought the car thief. Prominent warnings are displayed in car parks, but still cameras and other valuables are left exposed to attract the opportunist felon. If you can't take your valuables with you, at least put them out of sight.

PUBLIC ACCESS

For the sake of completeness, I have included in this book many tarns that are on agricultural or private land, or are inaccessible to the general public for some other reason. Such tarns are recorded on the Ordnance Survey map anyway, so there is no point in trying to conceal them. Accessibility is clearly stated in the main text and noted in the alphabetical list on p. 217.

At the time of writing, Local Authorities throughout the country – assisted by various interested bodies such as the Groundwork Trust and the Ramblers Association – are actively engaged in 'Recreation 2000', a Government-sponsored programme to identify and mark all public footpaths. The project involves defining rights of way (now shown on Ordnance Survey maps by green pecked lines) by means of waymarking and the erection of finger posts. This work has already been completed within the Lake District National Park.

In all cases where routes have been given in the text I have walked these myself and believe them to be public rights of way, as defined on the Ordnance Survey maps used.

WALKING TIMES

The tarns are graded for accessibility, according to surrounding terrain and distance from the nearest public road, in the alphabetical list on p. 217. Where necessary, at the end of the tarn description in the main text I have given approximate walking times for the outward journey only, making a generous allowance for walkers of differing ability. This does not include stops for snacks, photography, removing boots to attend to blisters, or other diversions.

EQUIPMENT

Boots are essential, not only to cope with rough ground on the fells but for muddy paths on lower ground. Windproof clothing is also a must, but need not be colourful and expensive to be effective. The important thing is its ability to prevent the loss of body heat. Two or three light woollen pullovers worn beneath a windproof outer layer are better than one thick jersey.

A guidebook is, of course, no substitute for map and compass. Once the guidebook route has been lost, only the map and compass – or good luck – can get you back on course.

MAPS

The book is divided into six sections based on the regions covered by the Ordnance Survey maps. Most of the tarns are located on the four Outdoor Leisure 1:25,000 maps, numbers 4–7; those which lie outside the areas covered by the Leisure maps are located on the Landranger 1:50,000 maps, numbers 90 and 96. The Ordnance Survey map used is indicated on the key map introducing each region.

Within each region, the tarns have been blocked into convenient areas, designated A, B, C, and so on. These area divisions are based on the accessibility and proximity of the tarns to each other.

The entry for each tarn is headed with some basic information. Tarn names are printed in capitals, and alternative names, where they exist, are given in lower case type. The Ordnance Survey grid reference appears next, followed by altitude, and approximate maximum depth if known. Surface areas are not included but a glance at the map will give some indication of relative size.

The Tarns of South-East Lakeland

The south-east region contains the largest number of recorded Cumbrian water bodies – a total of 85. Here are highland tarns of ridge and shelf formation and lowland tarns with enriched waters abounding in aquatic plants, as well as reed fen and willow and alder carr developments.

The rocks underlying much of South-East Lakeland are the comparatively softer Silurian Slates which have weathered to produce a gentler and less elevated terrain than that found elsewhere in Lakeland, making this ideal walking country for all abilities. In the northern section of the key map (Areas I and J) the country becomes more rugged; the tarns of Scandale and Red Screes above the Kirkstone Pass, and particularly Greycrag Tarn above Longsleddle, are especially demanding.

Grasmere, Ambleside and Windermere are probably the busiest parts of Lakeland during the tourist season. To avoid the crowds, take to the tarns!

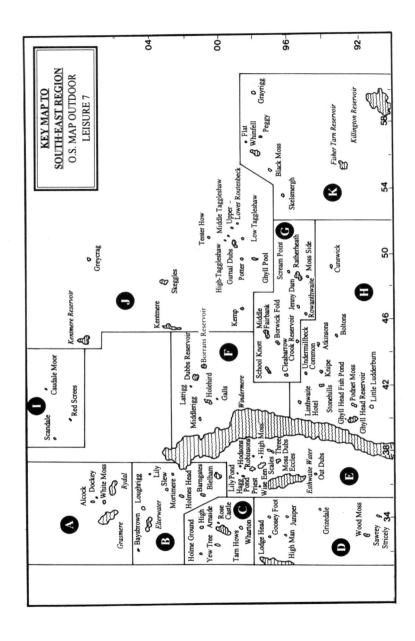

04

00

96

92

A

Grasmere
Alcock
Dockey
White Moss
Rydal
Baysbrown
Loughrigg
Lily
Ellerwater
Slew
Mortimere

B
Holmes Head
Barngates
Blelham
Rose Castle
High Arnside
Yew Tree
Holme Ground

C
Tarn Hows
Wharton
Lily Pond
Hagg
Pond
Hodsons
Robinsons
Priest
Wise Een
Scales
Three
Moss Dubs
Eccles
High Moss

D
Lodge Head
Goosey Foot
High Man
Juniper
Grizedale
Wood Moss
Sawrey
Stricely
34

E
Esthwaite Water
Out Dubs
38

Scandale
Caudale Moor
Red Screes

I

Greycrag

Latrigg
Middlerigg
Holehird
Galls
Windermere

Skeggles
Kentmere

J

Kentmere Reservoir

Dubbs Reservoir
Borrans Reservoir

F
School Knott
Middle
Fairbank
Cleabarrow
Borwick Fold
Crook Reservoir
Jenny Dam
Undermillbeck
Common
Atkinsons
Knipe
Stonehills
Linthwaite
Hotel
Ghyll Head Fish Pond
Podnet Moss
Ghyll Head Reservoir
Little Ludderburn
Kemp

High Tagglesbaw
Gurnal Dubs
Potter
Ghyll Pool
Low Tagglesbaw
Middle Tagglesbaw
Upper –
Lower Routenbeck
Tenter How

G
Scream Point
Ratherheath
Rowanthwaite
Moss Side
Curswick

H
Boltons

Flat
Whinfell
Peggy
Black Moss
Graynig

K
Skelsmergh
Fisher Tarn Reservoir
Killington Reservoir

58

54

50

46

42

Area A

WHITE MOSS TARN

Grid reference: 347068	Altitude: 114m (375ft)	Depth: 1m (3ft)

Between the lakes of Grasmere and Rydal Water the A591 skirts
an area of rising ground, wooded and quarried, known as White
Moss Common. Across the common runs the track of the old
coffin road from Rydal, for the rocky ground at Rydal Church
was never consecrated. This is why the Wordsworth family graves
are to be found in Grasmere Churchyard even though they died at
Rydal Mount.

Beside the track, tarmacked at this point, lies White Moss Tarn,
described by Heaton Cooper as a 'small reedy pool'. In spring,
edged with rush, pierced by water horsetail and set about by
birch, alder and brilliant copper beech, this elongated tarn is quite
beautiful. Later in the year, water horsetail predominates and little
of the water surface can be seen. A small beck flows in from the
west and the outflow passes beneath the road to join the water
which eventually falls into the disused quarry, now a car park,
below.

Across the road one may wander by numerous paths to the
viewpoint on White Moss Common, passing on the way the
infilled and overgrown remains of a lost tarn tucked between
rocky, ice-smoothed knolls. Somewhere on this rocky knoll of
knolls is a small, tree-fringed pond of cool water, surrounded by
the remains of iron railings. Whirligig beetles chase across the
surface of what was once a small private reservoir. Oak, birch,
alder and sycamore were deliberately planted to shade it. It is
probably spring-fed, as there is no inlet stream. (*About 10 minutes
by the track from the car park*.) **See Walk 2**.

ALCOCK TARN

Grid reference: 349079	Altitude: 365m (1,190ft)	Depth: 2m (6½ft)

This was originally a small natural water known as Butter Crags
Tarn. It was enlarged by the building of a stone and earth dam and

stocked with brown trout by a Mr Alcock of the Hollins, Grasmere, late in the nineteenth century. Situated on a narrow shelf above the village, it is overshadowed by the crags from which it derived its original name. The tarn itself, if plain and somewhat lacking in character, is far enough off the beaten track to offer refuge from the madding crowd, and well worth the climb for the extensive views it offers to the south and west. Here in summer will be found a range of aquatic plants including water horsetail, floating pondweed, and near the dam some fine floating bur-reed.

To reach the tarn, take the minor road off the A591, travel past Dove Cottage and for some distance uphill, then bear left past Wishing Gate House, then left again beside the seat and along the broad signposted track. Here one is faced with two alternatives: left through the gate and past a small artificial pond, an easy winding ascent; or right, by a rather steeper track. Both ways lead to the tarn. After visiting the tarn, continue north along the track to descend beside Greenhead Gill. (You may notice the bridge across the beck – it carries the conduit from Thirlmere to Manchester.) Continue down the metalled lane to arrive eventually beside the Swan Hotel at the north end of the village. (*Alcock Tarn is about 45–60 minutes from Dove Cottage. To visit White Moss Tarn first, continue eastwards along the metalled road, past Wishing Gate House, for 3 minutes.*) **See Walk 2.**

DOCKEY TARN

Grid reference: 354073	Altitude: 385m (1,260ft)	Depth: 1m (3ft)

This tiny tarn lies at nearly the same altitude as Alcock Tarn, some 500m (550yds) to the south-east. There is no clear track, nor can the tarn be seen until one is close by. In summer the walk is made more difficult by dense bracken, but by following sheep trods and keeping to the same contour of the hill on the narrowing shelf, one will eventually light upon it. Here is the charm and mild excitement of tarn hunting, and the sense of achievement one feels on finally discovering an elusive pond. Dockey Tarn nestles against a bright grassy mound, topped by a small rock outcrop and set about by grey boulders. It has a rocky bottom and abounds in water starwort. From its edge Alcock Tarn can just be seen. (*About 15–20 minutes from Alcock Tarn.*) **See Walk 2.**

Dockey Tarn   This pretty water hides from all but the dedicated tarn-hunter.

Area B

BAYSBROWN TARN

Grid reference: 317048	Altitude: 45m (148ft)	Depth: 1m (3ft)

This man-made tarn stands at the edge of agricultural land and just off the bridleway that runs roughly north-west from Elterwater village through Baysbrown Woods, paralleling the Great Langdale Beck. It is a substantial, froggy pond, edged by sedge and rush, and containing a dense growth of broad-leaved pondweed. There is no positive inflow but, judging by the strong outflow at the right-hand end of the earth dam, there must be considerable drainage from the surrounding area in wet weather. The glint of its water can be seen through the trees on the north side of the bridleway. (*From Elterwater village allow 30–45 minutes.*)

LOUGHRIGG TARN

Grid reference: 345044	Altitude: 94m (310ft)	Depth: 12m (39ft)

This is a water of outstanding beauty, due to its almost circular form, its striking views north-west towards the Langdale Pikes, and the variety of aquatic plants which adorn its margins. William Wordsworth's description of the tarn in his *Guide through the District of the Lakes*, published in 1810, still cannot be bettered:

Of this class of miniature lakes, Loughrigg Tarn near Grasmere is the most beautiful example. It has a margin of green firm meadows, of rocks, and rocky woods, a few reeds here, a little company of waterlilies there, with beds of gravel or stone beyond; a tiny stream issuing neither briskly nor sluggishly out of it; but its feeding rills, from the shortness of their course, so small as to be scarcely visible. Five or six cottages are reflected in its peaceful bosom; rocky and barren steeps rise up above the hanging enclosures; and the solemn pikes at Langdale overlook, from a distance, the low cultivated ridge of land that forms the northern boundary of this small, quiet and fertile domain.

(There may be parking space near Tarn Foot, from whence a public footpath encircles that part of the tarn not bordered by the road. About 5–10 minutes from the road.)

LILY TARN

Grid reference: 364040	Altitude: 200m (654ft)	Depth: 1m (3ft)

This is a misnomer – or at least it was at the time of my visit. Better by far the boggy pond which I passed some 200m (220yds) before reaching Lily Tarn, and which was ablaze with fine, white, waxy blooms. There, too, were cotton grass and darting dragon flies. Lily Tarn itself was much overgrown with rush and sedge but its lilies were somewhat sparse. During the Second World War this tarn is said to have been stocked with carp; if they were still there they remained aloof.

At Clappersgate there is a convenient car park beside the River Brathay. Re-cross the road bridge to the junction where a steep, walled track ascends to the left of the telephone kiosk. The track emerges on to open hillside and winds steeply up to the undulating plateau that is Loughrigg Fell. There are a number of unnamed natural tarns in the area, of which Lily Tarn is the largest.

Extensive views down the length of Windermere can be enjoyed from beside the water. (*Allow 45 minutes from the road.*)

SLEW TARN

Grid reference: 356030	Altitude: 55m (180ft)	Depth: 2m (6½ft)

Hidden in the bluebell woodland around Skelwith Fold is this tree-shrouded, lily-dappled, iris-edged water where the filtered sunshine sparkles on the smooth surface. It was probably originally a small, natural tarn which was enlarged to form an ornamental fish pond for the owner of the big house, now the offices of the Skelwith Fold Caravan Park. There is no public access except for caravanners staying within the grounds.

MORTIMERE

Grid reference: 364029	Altitude: 55m (180ft)	Depth: 2m (6½ft)

About 500m (550yds) south of the Brathay Bridge at Clappersgate, beside the B5286 road to Hawkshead, this artificial tarn can just be seen within the grounds of Brathay Hall. The Brathay Hall Field Study Centre was established in the 1960s to provide field training for students of geology, geography and biology. The Director of Studies at the time was Mike Mortimer. In order to provide a handy site for biological studies, Mike enlarged a small existing pond with the aid of 'A' level students and the occasional mechanical digger. At one time golden orfe were introduced but when it became overstocked the fish were cleared. Sadly Mike died in 1983 but the pond, now recorded on the Ordnance Survey map, remains as a lasting memorial to a man who devoted his life to his students.

HOLMES HEAD TARN

Grid reference: 351024	Altitude: 105m (345ft)	Depth: 2m (6½ft)

To find this tarn, branch west off the B5286 at Clappersgate on to Bog Lane. Then, some 500m (550yds) south of Skelwith Fold, take a gated track signed to Holmes Head Farm. Beside the track, some 150m (163yds) from the road, is Holmes Head Tarn where one may gaze at but not approach the shoals of golden orfe which feed near the edge. The tarn is shallow and artificial but may be an enlargement of a small natural water; one can never be sure. This pretty pond, formed in the 1930s, is private, as is the fishing. On a later visit in early spring, the tarn was presided over by a large, grey heron which flapped heavily away at my approach. (*About 15 minutes along the track from the road.*)

BARNGATES TARN (Drunken Duck) and WATER BARNETTS TARN

Grid reference: 351011	Altitude: 122m (400ft)	Depth: 9m (29½ft)

Barngates Tarn is an artificial water constructed in the 1930s to supply water to the Drunken Duck Inn and for use as a fish pond. Now stocked with brown and rainbow trout, it provides excellent fishing. It is also a very beautiful water, its bays and promontories being set about with a variety of plant life. Nowadays the inn obtains its water from a new reservoir higher up the hillside. The tarn lies across the road from the inn.

Immediately behind the Drunken Duck is another small pond, also used for fishing. This was formed from a boggy patch in 1980–1 and is linked to its larger neighbour by a small stream along which trout have migrated. The new water is called Water Barnetts, an old name resurrected from the 1824 deeds relating to the inn.

This must be one of the best fishing spots in Lakeland, combining fine fish, fine beers and fine cuisine.

BLELHAM TARN

Grid reference: 366005	Altitude: 43m (138ft)	Depth: 4m (13ft)

Situated on National Trust property, this sizeable lowland water seems more like a lake than a tarn. Access is by way of a public footpath which extends from the B5286 Ambleside to Hawkshead road just north of Outgate. Blelham Tarn is not as visually impressive as the higher tarns in my opinion, and the moods of the water respond easily to the weather. Fishing is permitted if you can overcome the barrier of the reed beds.

This tarn has made an important contribution to our knowledge of the evolution of the environment since the last Ice Age. By analysing pollen grains taken from the tarn bed and its associated bog, researchers have been able to build up a fairly accurate picture of changes in vegetation cover since the ice receded, together with indications of changes in climate and, to some extent, the influence wrought by prehistoric dwellers on their surroundings. (*About 10–15 minutes from the road.*)

Area C

HIGH ARNSIDE TARN

Grid reference: 331012	Altitude: 175m (574ft)	Depth: 3m (10ft)

Here I met two anglers one May morning; the elder claimed to have rodded every Lakeland tarn containing trout. At his feet lay a

High Arnside Tarn   Despite the weeds this water offers good fishing.

fine 1kg (2lb) rainbow – and an open box with an assortment of flies, the like of which I had never seen. This is an entirely artificial water with a long, low dam across the southern end; it was built by James Marshall of Coniston who was also responsible for the creation of Tarn Hows to the south.

Sedge and pondweed are steadily encroaching at the northern and eastern sides of the tarn, but the fishing, by fly only, is obviously still plentiful. It is controlled by the Windermere, Ambleside and District Angling Association. To the east rises the steep wooded hillside of Arnside Intake, and trees surround the tarn to the north.

The path which skirts the western shore of Tarn Hows continues northwards as the Cumbria Way, passes High Arnside Tarn, and continues to the A593 Coniston to Skelwith Bridge Road at High Cross. (*From High Cross, the tarn is 15–20 minutes walk.*) **See Walk 4.**

TARN HOWS (Highlow Tarn, The Tarns)

Grid reference: 331000	Altitude: 188m (618ft)	Depth: 9m (29½ft)

This large, artificial tarn of chocolate-box charm is a well-known tourist trap. Its great popularity is probably due to its accessibility by car (there is a large but expensive car park nearby), the beautiful composition of its trees, hillsides and water when viewed from above, its deeply indented shoreline of bays and promontories, and its several islands. Friendly footpaths lead the visitor through this wonderland, offering fresh views around every bend without overtaxing seldom-used muscles.

Tarn Hows was formed from three natural tarns – hence the alternative names – by means of a small dam built in the early years of this century. (A broader dam has since been added, in front of the original one, to take the heavier foot traffic.) The tarn and its surroundings were given to the National Trust through the influence and generosity of Beatrix Potter.

Owing to the narrow approach roads and the volume of traffic, a one-way system was introduced in the 1960s. The approach is from High Cross or Hawkshead Hill from the B5285 Coniston to Hawkshead Road. **See Walk 4.**

ROSE CASTLE TARN (Plantation Tarn)

Grid reference: 334002	Altitude: 191m (626ft)	Depth: 2m (6½ft)

This tarn is so close to Tarn Hows that a casual glance at the map might lead one to believe that it was part and parcel of that larger water. In fact it is quite separate, lying on the eastern side of Tarn Hows, about 3m (10ft) above it. Immediately around the tarn is a wildlife conservation area, fortunately seldom visited by the thousands of visitors who annually perambulate around the main pathways. A shack with a hide beside it overlooks the smaller tarn, which has an abundance of yellow water lily, broad-leaved pondweed and, at the south-east corner, bogbean. A short ½m (1½ft) high concrete dam holds the tarn, the surplus water trickling over into Tarn Hows.

WHARTON TARN (High Cross Tarn)

Grid reference: 331988	Altitude: 179m (585ft)	Depth: 2m (6½ft)

Approximately 200m (220yds) north-west of High Cross, on the B5285 Hawkshead to Coniston road, is Wharton Tarn. It lies within a shallow basin between low rock outcrops and residual moraine where it is fed by three short streams. The water seems to have been partially drained at one time, for a straight ditch, now dry and choked with weeds, runs from the tarn across the neighbouring field.

The broad marshy area on the tarn's east side, now overgrown with sweet-smelling bog myrtle (or sweet gale), is probably a result of this partial draining. This shrub merges into a narrow belt of carr interspersed with willow and alder. On higher ground, spaced silver birch stand sentinel before the tarn; behind, the rising hillside of mixed woodland completes the setting of this lovely, natural water. An unworked roadside quarry, now used for storing council road metal, provides limited parking. From here, a short uphill walk reveals a ladder stile on the left where a waymarked path leads to the tarn.

It is haunted, 'tis said, by an old woman of unwholesome appearance – hence the almost forgotten local name 'Jenny Greenteeth Tarn'. (*About 2 minutes from the stile.*)

YEW TREE TARN

Grid reference: 322004	Altitude: 105m (344ft)	Depth: 3m (10ft)

Probably the most accessible tarn in Lakeland; one may park on the layby beside it and gaze over the wall at its beauty without even leaving one's seat. The landowner James Marshall built a dam at the south end in the 1930s and stocked the tarn with trout. Brown and rainbow varieties can be had by the angler; and the fishing is controlled by the Coniston and Torver Angling Association. It is possible to make a circuit of the water by crossing the dam, but the northern end can be very boggy.

The tarn is the property of the National Trust, and lies beside the A593, halfway between Coniston and Skelwith Bridge. **See Walk 4.**

Yew Tree Tarn   Tall conifers stand sentinel on the northern shore.

HOLME GROUND TARNS

Grid references: 315011 & 316011	Altitude: 225m (738ft)	Depth: 2m (6½ft)

This is yet another artificial tarn – or pair of reservoirs to be precise – on the opposite side of Holme Fell, and north-west from Yew Tree Tarn. These reservoirs were originally formed to provide water for the slate quarries nearby: a water-filled skip would descend, drawing up another one loaded with hewn slate. When the latter had been unloaded, the role of counterweight would be reversed. This scheme operated well until the quarry pit was worked below the level at which the water could be drained away. At that point a steam engine had to be installed. The water-filled quarry can be seen at 316017, a little way north along the track from the tarns.

The larger of the two reservoirs has matured into a tarn-like feature and is well worth visiting in its lovely setting. The smaller is held by four stone-faced earth dams, two at the head and two at the foot. Access by car is difficult; perhaps the best bet is to use the car park at Low Tilberthwaite (308009), then follow the directions given at the end of Walk 4, page 188. (*Allow 45–60 minutes.*)

Area D

The Tarns of Grizedale Forest

South of Hawkshead, and between Coniston and Windermere, is an area of high ground known as Grizedale Forest, managed since 1937 by the Forestry Commission but with a history of woodland use going back some 500 years. Within the forest are 15 or more tarns of varying sizes, some natural, some artificial, some to which the public have access and some where access is restricted on the grounds of conservation, woodland safety, or because they are used as bird sanctuaries. A number of these ponds were created by the raising of simple earth mounds to impound water, presumably in case of forest fire. Others predate the present forest management.

The public may visit the following tarns using paths within the Forestry Commission Woodland. Useful maps of the forest and its tracks are available from the Grizedale Visitors' Centre, formerly Grizedale Hall.

JUNIPER TARN

Grid reference: 339964	Altitude: 206m (676ft)	Depth: 0.5m (2ft)

From Hawkshead, take the minor road on the west side of Esthwaite Water. Then, just 400m (440yds) after leaving the village, take the right turn uphill for Grizedale and Satterthwaite. The first car park on the right on entering the forest (344966) provides easy access to both Juniper and Goosey Foot Tarns. The Ordnance Survey map or the Forestry Commission's own Grizedale Forest Guide Map will help you locate Juniper Tarn.

This small water was enclosed within a man-high chainlink fence when I first visited, but this has now been removed. A low earth dam with wood supports retains the pond. Broadleaved pondweed grows here, and pond skaters abound. Ashore, yellow flag iris trim the margin, while rhododendron and tall conifers press in closely all around.

In the early years of this century the tarn was used by a Mr Brocklebank, a ship-owner and former owner of the estate, to sail steam-driven model boats. They would be tethered to a post in the centre of the tarn and made to circle slowly round. (*From the car park, allow 15 minutes.*)

GOOSEY FOOT TARN (Guinea Hill Tarn)

Grid reference: 338970	Altitude: 244m (800ft)	Depth: 2.5m (8ft)

Once used as a reservoir for Hawkshead, this long, narrow, artificial water, sited in a shallow vale, is impounded by a low concrete dam at each end. The outflow is at the northern end and water filters in from the surrounding marsh.

With autumn sunlight shining through the mist, and the surrounding conifers reflected in its surface, Goosey Foot Tarn is indeed a magical place. Beside the tarn a sign once explained its intended purpose – the encouragement of wildfowl and especially the resettlement of greylag geese. The sign has now been removed; perhaps the geese omitted to read it.

The tarn lies north of Juniper Tarn; to find it, check your map with care. (*About 20 minutes walk from the car park at 344966.*)

GRIZEDALE TARN

Grid reference: 346944	Altitude: 207m (680ft)	Depth: 2m (6½ft)

About 1km (½ mile) due east of the Grizedale Forest Visitors' Centre (where there are large car parks) is Grizedale Tarn and its two satellite tarns. Waymarked paths on the Silurian Way lead to this Shangri La hidden in the forest.

The tarns are located on a level, marshy saddle where the main outflow runs west to the Grizedale Valley, and that from the eastern tarn goes towards the Dale Beck on the opposite side of the ridge. The main tarn is overlooked on the north side by a low escarpment of Silurian rock; projecting into the water from a causeway on the west side is a timber observation platform. This charming, natural tarn provided an emergency water supply for Grizedale Hall during the Second World War, when the building was used as an officers' POW camp. (*About 40 minutes from the road.*)

The other four tarns of significance within the forest have little charm, except perhaps for Wood Moss, but in any case they are on private Forestry Commission land, and therefore inaccessible to the general public. They are listed below.

LODGE HEAD TARN

Grid reference: 327972	Altitude: 238m (781ft)	Depth: 2m (6½ft)

The surface of this dreary tree-shrouded pond is covered with broadleaved pondweed. It has a simple earth dam through which a small stream flows away towards Coniston.

HIGH MAN TARN

Grid reference: 329965	Altitude: 261m (857ft)	Depth: 2m (6½ft)

Another dull pond, tree-fringed and with a single island, this is the source of Grizedale Beck. When visited, the surface was half covered with broadleaved pondweed and sparsely edged with sedge and rush. A mallard drake and solitary chick were the only occupants – perhaps mother was still sitting somewhere on the central island.

SAWREY STRICELEY

Grid reference: 339907	Altitude: 55m (180ft)	Depth: 2m (6½ft)

The name suggests a tarn of some elegance and character, but alas, it turns out to be another artificial water with an earth dam. The surrounding broadleaved woodland, extensive sedge and the presence of a few yellow flag iris make it slightly more interesting than its sisters listed above; presumably it benefits from the less rigorous weather conditions of a lower altitude. Springs and seepage raise the water level, while the surplus runs off to join Force Beck. Despite the seclusion and security offered by the presence of two islands, no waterfowl appear to have settled here as yet.

WOOD MOSS TARN (Hob Gill Tarn)

Grid reference: 328918	Altitude: 155m (508ft)	Depth: 3m (10ft)

Of all the tarns in Grizedale this is by far the largest and provides sanctuary during spring and early summer for myriad wheeling black-headed gulls engaged in noisy domestic discourse. Two hides have been erected on the eastern shore overlooking the tarn and information regarding the facilities and permission to visit the site can be obtained through the Forestry Information Shop at Grizedale.

Several small islands provide secure nesting sites; while, on the shore, red squirrels may be encountered. Hob Gill flows through the tarn, then steeply down to join Force Beck.

Area E

Claife Heights

Between Esthwaite Water and Windermere there is an undulating ridge of high ground extending north to south, generally known as Claife Heights. Latterbarrow, the highest point, is located at the northern end. The land is owned variously by the National Trust, the Forestry Commission, farms and estates.

Within this upland area are 11 named tarns, only six of which are accessible by public rights of way. Most have been rejuvenated by damming and some have been used as experimental waters by the Freshwater Biological Association based at Far Sawrey. Claife Heights may be reached by footpaths starting from Far Sawrey and Near Sawrey in the south, from High Wray in the north, and from Colthouse in the west. **See Walk 3.**

--------- *Accessible Claife Heights Tarns* ---------

MOSS ECCLES TARN

Grid reference: 372968	Altitude: 166m (544ft)	Depth: 5m (15ft)

Popular with anglers and walkers alike, this tarn is held by two short dams located on either side of a huge rock outcrop. The tree-fringed western arm is ablaze with water lilies in their season, creating a display which far surpasses any artificial water garden. The main body of the tarn is more open, set against varying shades of green, from the darkest woodland to the bright emerald of rolling grassland. It is a Site of Special Scientific Interest.

Beatrix Potter once kept a rowing boat here and used this tarn and neighbouring Esthwaite Water as the setting for her *Tale of Jeremy Fisher*.

Fishing for trout, perch, eels and pike is controlled by the Windermere Ambleside and District Angling Association. Footpaths northwards from Near and Far Sawrey lead to the tarn. (*Allow about 30–45 minutes from either village.*) **See Walk 3.**

WISE EEN TARN

Grid reference: 370976	Altitude: 196m (643ft)	Depth: 5m (15ft) est.

The footpath northwards from Moss Eccles leads one past this rather larger tarn where fishing is not permitted. In clear weather it is a superb viewpoint; to the north and west stretches a panorama from the Coniston to the Langdale Fells. A large earthern dam at the north end holds the tarn; adjacent to it is a large timber boathouse. (*About 10 minutes from Moss Eccles.*) See **Walk 3**.

SCALE HEAD TARN

Grid reference: 373975	Altitude: 200m (656ft)	Depth: 2m (6½ft)

Beside Wise Een, on the opposite side of the path, is Scale Head Tarn. A concrete dam retains this water which now bears an extensive growth of pondweed and sedge. Whatever its former purpose may have been, this is now redundant. See **Walk 3**.

HIGH MOSS TARN

Grid reference: 375980	Altitude: 225m (738ft)	Depth: 1m (3ft)

A most disappointing water this, being almost entirely overgrown with sedge and rush. It lies beside the footpath which comes from Wise Een and Scale Head Tarns. (*About 10 minutes*). See **Walk 3**.

BROWNSTONE TARN

Grid reference: 383976	Altitude: 238m (780ft)	Depth: 1m (3ft)

I accidentally stumbled on this small artificial pond while walking Claife Heights. Its name was painted on a stone slab beside the tarn. See **Walk 3**.

LILY POND

Grid reference: 367984	Altitude: 194m (636ft)	Depth: 0.5m (2ft)

Beside the footpath that originates just north of Colthouse and runs in an easterly direction towards the forest is this shallow, overgrown pond, now practically devoid of lilies but surrounded by rhododendrons. (*Allow 25 minutes from Colthouse.*)

Inaccessible Claife Heights Tarns

WRAYMIRES TARN

Grid reference: 369979	Altitude: 185m (607ft)	Depth: 3m (10ft) est.

A very pretty water this, just north of Wise Een, held by an earth dam and surrounded on three sides by conifer plantations. The hurricanes of spring 1990 transformed the mature plantation to the west of the tarn into a strange, horizontal forest – an almost impenetrable tangle of trunks and roots.

ROBINSON'S TARN

Grid reference: 369981	Altitude: 188m (617ft)	Depth: Nil

Some 200m (220yds) north of Wraymires, Robinson's Tarn is a patch of mud and vegetation with very little standing water remaining. It seems strange that the Ordnance Survey should name this marshy patch and leave Hodson's Tarn – a little further north-west – unnamed.

HODSON'S TARN

Grid reference: 369982	Altitude: 195m (640ft)	Depth: 3m (10ft) est.

By the late 1930s this tarn had degenerated into a marsh but it was revived in 1955 by the building of an earth and stone dam for the Freshwater Biological Association. Latent aquatic vegetation recolonised the tarn which subsequently became the scene of pioneering work in freshwater biology, including studies of the feeding habits of the brown trout.

The tarn is confined between gentle slopes of conifer woodland, and rhododendrons edge the western shore.

HAGG POND

Grid reference: 367983	Altitude: 190m (623ft)	Depth: 1m (3ft)

Two tiny linked tarns, almost squeezed out of existence by encroaching rhododendrons and other vegetation, exist nose-to-tail so to speak, to the west of Hodson's Tarn. They are held by a small concrete dam incorporating a sluice.

THREE DUBS

Grid reference: 378974	Altitude: 206m (676ft)	Depth: 5m (16½ft) est.

Behind a buttressed concrete dam with a sluice stands this tranquil water – perhaps, as the name suggests, formed from three smaller ponds. Beside the dam and projecting into the water is a quaint two-storey building with an oriel window overlooking the tarn. At the opposite end of the water a rock ridge inclines steeply to the tarn basin which is in turn flanked by tall conifers.

Like Hodson's, Three Dubs has been used for freshwater biological research.

Tarns of the Esthwaite Water Basin

Two lowland tarns share the Esthwaite glacial basin: Priest Pot to the north of the lake and Out Dubs Tarn to the south. They were probably both part of the main body of the lake at one time. Each of these tarns is almost entirely surrounded by marshland and dense willow and alder carr, so that little of the open water can be seen from the nearest public access.

PRIEST POT

Grid reference: 357978	Altitude: 66m (216ft)	Depth: 4m (13ft) est.

Priest Pot is located at the northern end of Esthwaite Water and is believed to have been cut off from the main body of water by the development of reed fen. This occurs when silt washed in by streams – in this case by Black Beck – gets trapped in the roots of the common reed, gradually transforming open water into marsh. Storm-blown debris from reed beds along the lake shore, driven northwards by the prevailing wind into the narrowing neck of the lake, may have played a part in sealing off the embryo tarn. Grasses, shrubs, willow and alder would eventually have gained a foothold in the advancing marsh to form carr.

Priest Pot is said to have been a fish pond for the monks at Furness Abbey and later served the same purpose for the occupants of Hawkshead Hall.

A good view of the surrounding carr – and a glimpse of the water – can be had from the A5285 Hawkshead to Far Sawrey road, but there is no public access across the agricultural land that surrounds it.

OUT DUBS TARN

Grid reference: 366948	Altitude: 62m (203ft)	Depth: 3m (10ft)

In contrast to Priest Pot, Out Dubs is separated from the lake not by fen carr, but by sediments. These sediments may be of glacial origin; certainly the peaty nature of the soil indicates that a tract of marsh once existed between the lake and the tarn. Perhaps Out Dubs was always a pond in its own right: a swelling in Cunsey Beck?

The tarn is best seen from the air, or in an aerial photograph, whereby the zoning of the aquatic plants can really be appreciated. From the central area of open water towards the shoreline, concentric zones of plants adapt to the varying depths. First, in the deeper central water, are the yellow water lilies. These are surrounded by belts of common reed, then sedges and grasses and finally willow carr.

The best ground view of the tarn can be had from the single track road on the east side which passes Dub How Farm. In early summer a sign warns motorists to beware of toads.

Area F

The following six waters occur in the area around Troutbeck Bridge between Ambleside and Windermere town, where the surrounding fells dip towards the north-eastern shore of the lake.

HOLEHIRD TARN

Grid reference: 409008	Altitude: 110m (361ft)	Depth: 3m (10ft) est.

It is surprising how few local residents, let alone visitors, are aware of the lovely gardens maintained by the Lakeland Horti-cultural Society (LHS) on the Holehird Estate. The house itself,

Holehird Tarn Yellow lilies and flag iris grace this artificial water.

the Holehird Cheshire Home for the disabled, is barred to the general public, but the tarn and grounds are accessible.

The estate is clearly signposted from the A592 north of Windermere and the car park is a few metres beyond the entrance on the left. From here a muddy path leads through a shrubbery to the tarn.

The tarn is wholly artificial, being held by a concrete dam backed by stone and earth. Constructed in the latter half of the nineteenth century as an ornamental pond during the landscaping of the original gardens, its sinuous curves are edged by iris, reedmace (bulrush), and yellow water lilies in their season.

The water may also be of interest to coarse fishermen; tickets may be obtained from the LHS office.

Afterwards, a visit to the gardens is highly recommended. Continue along the drive, bearing right to the LHS car park. Do not call at the lodge, nor at the mansion; large or noisy parties are not welcome. Information on the house and grounds can be gleaned from the LHS publications available at their offices by the gardens.

MIDDLERIGG TARN

Grid reference: 397011	Altitude: 84m (275ft)	Depth: 3m (10ft)

This tarn is situated on private property, though it can easily be seen from the bridleway which passes nearby.

As with Holehird, this is another possible combination visit. You can begin by calling in at Brockhole and enjoying the facilities of the Visitors' Centre. Then turn right outside Brockhole and walk along the A591 for some 300m (330yds) to the signposted bridleway of Wain Lane. The tarn, which is artificial, is held by an earth and stone dam at the south end. It is a fine, broad ornamental pond with swans a-swimming and fish a-leaping and contains a small island. If you're in the mood for proper exercise, continue uphill to the road, turn left along it for some 400m (440yds), then take the next bridleway left (Mirk Lane) which will take you back to within a few paces of the Brockhole entrance. (*Allow 1 hour for the round trip.*)

LATRIGG TARN

Grid reference: 417018	Altitude: 245m (805ft)	Depth: 2m (6½ft)

This is a small artificial pond on private ground, which can barely be seen from the Longmire Road. Overshadowed on the western side by trees, it is a rather featureless fish pond.

BORRANS RESERVOIR

Grid reference: 429010	Altitude: 198m (649ft)	Depth: 6m (19½ft) est.

DUBBS RESERVOIR (Windermere Reservoir)

Grid reference: 422018	Altitude: 228m (748ft)	Depth: 4.5m (15ft) est.

Some 700m (770yds) to the east, and parallel with the Longmire Road, is Dubbs Road, a similar bridle track. The reservoirs are situated on either side of this road and are the property of North

West Water. Borrans is the more picturesque of the two, but neither rate as 'tarns'. They are mentioned only because they are recorded as substantial bodies of water in this area. Dubbs Reservoir is also a trout fishery and may be taken in as part of an excellent circular walk – or mountain bike ride.

Start from the Moorhowe Road, which links the A591 near Ings with the A592 south of Troutbeck. There is limited parking at the start of Dubbs Road. About 1km (½mile) north-west of Ings along the Moorhowe Road, take the bridleway (435996) signposted northwards towards High House. Just after the sharp right-hand bend beyond this farm, turn left and northwards again to cross open moorland and descend to Kentmere. Return up the steep Crabtree Brow and over the Garburn Pass to Dubbs Road, taking the uphill fork to get to Moorhowe Road past Dubbs Reservoir. The total distance from Dubbs Road is about 13km (8miles). (*Allow 4–5 hours on foot; 3–4 hours for a novice on a mountain bike.*)

GALLS TARN

Grid reference: 409004	Altitude: 140m (459ft)	Depth: 1m (3ft)

Just south of Holehird Gardens on the A592 is St Anne's School for Girls. In the grounds at the back of the school, and named on the OS map, is Galls Tarn, a tiny elliptical puddle at the bottom of a 2m (6½ft) deep hole which looks like a long-disused stone quarry. Certainly the tarn has existed since the main house was built in the 1830s, but it is curious that so small a pond should be recorded; no one at the school could tell me why. There is no inflowing stream and it appears to rely on seepage from the high ground which rises directly to the east. In 1990 it was marginally reduced in size to accommodate the building of an all-weather hockey pitch.

The school grounds are of course private and the tarn is of little interest. When visited, it was partially covered by an algaic scum.

Area G

East of Bowness, and north of the B5284 road to Kendal, is an area of undulating pasture and moorland dotted with many small outcrops of Silurian rock and dried-up basins which, in very wet conditions, form temporary ponds. It is pleasant country, providing a contrast to the ruggedness of Lakeland proper; the single-track, tarmacked roads linking farm with farm are mainly unfenced and gated at intervals.

SCHOOL KNOTT TARN

Grid reference: 428973	Altitude: 198m (640ft)	Depth: 3m (10ft)

From the centre of Windermere town, this tarn lies about 1.6km (1mile) to the east, and judging by the well-used footpaths leading to it from that direction, it is popular with walkers. The approach from the east by the Dales Way path appears less frequented.

This delightful natural tarn lies on a gentle col between the opposing high ground of School Knott and Grandsire, and empties its waters through an artificially deepened channel down the valley towards the south-west. From its elevated situation there are extensive views towards the Kentmere and Longsleddale fells. A line of blasted conifers overlooks its southern shore. The tarn has a scoured, rocky bottom of some depth, and wave action driven by the prevailing winds has caused it to form a shallow reedy extension towards the north-east.

Fishing for the resident trout, by fly only, is controlled by the Windermere, Ambleside and District Angling Association. According to A. Wainwright, here be toads! (*Allow 45 minutes from Windermere.*) **See Walk 1.**

CLEABARROW TARN

Grid reference: 424963	Altitude: 168m (551ft)	Depth: 2.5m (8ft)

This attractive tarn is situated in a field close to the junction of the fell road from Ings with the B5284 Bowness to Crook road at Cleabarrow, opposite the Windermere Golf Course. Surrounded by a wire fence with stiles for access, the tarn lies barely 1.6km (1mile) south of School Knott Tarn, to which it is linked by footpaths.

Cleabarrow may have originally been a small natural tarn, and was probably enlarged to produce a sizeable fish pond. The fishing is currently controlled by the Windermere, Ambleside and District Angling Association and is said to include tench, carp, eels and some trout. The water is edged with sedge and rush, and at the time of my visit bunches of bright kingcups nodded to their reflections in the still water. The blades of flag iris speared upwards, and beyond, a solitary swan quietly explored the green depths with graceful thrusts of its neck. I glimpsed its mate later on, nesting on the largest of the three islands. (*From School Knott Tarn, allow 20–30 minutes.*) **See Walk 1.**

BORWICK FOLD TARN

Grid reference: 443969	Altitude: 195m (640ft)	Depth: 3m (10ft)

Borwick Fold, some 3.2km (2miles) south of Ings, is a pretty water with a smaller satellite tarn and a short channel linking the two. The main catchment for the tarns is a steep, wooded valley to the south. Coot and mallard were present and a pair of herons glided like blue-grey shadows over the site. The main tarn, held by a small dam, was constructed on a former swamp in the 1930s and stocked with trout. A notice on the locked gate indicates that the water is on private land, but it can easily be viewed from the roadside. The best overview may be had from the high ground opposite.

MIDDLE FAIRBANK TARN (Stewart's Reservoir)

Grid reference: 450973	Altitude: 198m (650ft)	Depth: 4m (13ft)

Across the road from Borwick Fold Tarn, and beside the unfenced road which runs south from Ings, is an area of high ground which overlooks Middle Fairbank Tarn and the surrounding countryside. This large artificial water, created from a former natural tarn by the raising of a 3m (9ft) high dam, is very open and somewhat featureless. When it was no longer required to supply water power for the bobbin mill at Staveley, it was stocked with trout for private fishing. From the tarn there are extensive views north and eastwards towards Kentmere, Longsleddale and the Howgills.

CROOK RESERVOIR

Grid reference: 445967	Altitude: 204m (670ft)	Depth: 3m (10ft) est.

One of several tarns in the rocky country which lies between Crook, Staveley and Windermere, Crook Reservoir is a former natural tarn with the level raised by a low stone and earth wall. Its function as a reservoir, if it ever was one, is long past; it is now a private fish pond, as we are reminded by a broken noticeboard nearby. There are three low, treeless islands and much bogbean in the shallows, while the margins are etched by dark rush. A swan and coot were in residence at the time of my visit and the somewhat dull landscape was brightened by bushes of bright yellow gorse.

From the B5284 Bowness to Kendal road, a signed footpath passes through Sunnybrow Farm and behind Boxtree Cottage, at which point a track extends north-west beside a beck which is the outflow from the tarn. This land is private property. There is also a small subsidiary tarn, much overgrown, to the south-west of the main water.

JENNY DAM (Green Hill Tarn)

Grid reference: 462965	Altitude: 135m (443ft)	Depth: 2m (6½ft) est.

This is an attractive little water poised in a rocky hollow above the village of Crook. However the approach, from the narrow road which extends north-west just to the west of the village, is now a smallholding and access is not encouraged by the occupier.

The surface of the water is mostly overgrown with the ubiquitous broadleaved pondweed but this did not deter the swan I saw with her five brown cygnets. It appears to be amply supplied from springs or by seepage and the small dam at the south-western end blends well with the natural surroundings. Considering the alternative name, it is probable that a small natural pond once existed here.

ROWANTHWAITE POND

Grid reference: 461963	Altitude: 98m (322ft)	Depth: 2m (6½ft) est.

There is no public access to this private pond but it may be glimpsed through the hedge which borders the B5284 road at Crook. It is an artificial water formed by the damming of two small becks flowing from the north.

RATHERHEATH TARN

Grid reference: 485959	Altitude: 106m (347ft)	Depth: 3.5m (11½ft)

A handy layby off the west-bound lane of the A591 provides access to Ashes Lane. Here a signed footpath traverses Rather Heath diagonally to the south-west, skirting the tarn and extending to Ratherheath Lane. A return eastwards along the lane

Ratherheath Tarn   A popular coarse fishery which echoes to the calls of coot and mallard.

provides another viewpoint. This is a curiously shaped double tarn which flanks either side of a wooded knoll; from no point can it be viewed as a whole.

The tarn belongs to the Cropper family (who own many ponds in the area) and is stocked for fishing which is now controlled by the Windermere, Ambleside and District Angling Association. New numbered fishing stations have recently been constructed and the tarn is available for coarse fishing except in April and May. Coot and swan find a haven here. (*About 20 minutes from the layby.*)

SCREAM POINT TARN

Grid reference: 484960	Altitude: 105m (344ft)	Depth: 1m (3ft)

Approximately 140m (152yds) north of Ratherheath Tarn is a long, narrow, muddy pond of no great interest except to the mother mallard I saw there with her five chicks.

A graveyard for dead and dying trees, the tarn lies beyond the public path on private ground.

MOSS SIDE TARN

Grid reference: 484956	Altitude: 105m (344ft)	Depth: 1m (3ft)

On the opposite side of Ratherheath Lane from Ratherheath Tarn a footpath runs south to Moss Side, passing near the tarn of that name. Sedge and rush have invaded, leaving little open water. The surrounding land is level and marshy, so the tarn is probably fairly shallow.

Area H

The tarns in this area are situated south of the B5284 Bowness to Kendal road, and east of Windermere, in country very similar to that north of the road. The exception is Cunswick Tarn near Kendal, at the foot of the limestone scarp of Cunswick Fell.

LINTHWAITE HOUSE HOTEL TARN

Grid reference: 407954	Altitude: 128m (420ft)	Depth: 3m (10ft)

The tarn belongs to the hotel and is a private water reserved for the enjoyment of guests staying at this very lovely house. As it does not appear on the Ordnance Survey map of 1907, it was probably constructed some time later as an artificial fish pond for the original owners of the house. The water is held by a substantial stone dam, grassed over, edged by trees and surrounded by delightful hillside gardens. Broadleaved pondweed, the principal vegetation, may be something of a hindrance to fly fishermen.

Linthwaite Tarn should not be confused with Lindeth Tarn which once existed nearby at 413947 but has sadly been filled in as a local refuse dump.

TARNS ON UNDERMILLBECK COMMON

Grid reference: 424951	Altitude: 156m (512ft)	Depth: 2m (6½ft) est.

These tarns are on private ground and there is no public access to them. Undermillbeck Common lies south of the Windermere Golf Course; it is a hummocky area of small rock outcrops and many boggy hollows, some of which retain small ponds. The largest of these, north-east of Barrow Plantation, is used for duck-rearing and for sporting purposes.

A footpath, indistinct but with stiles, leads from Lindeth Lane to Barrow plantation, but tarn-wise there is nothing of merit in this area.

STONEHILLS TARN (Barrow Plantation Tarn)

Grid reference: 417944	Altitude: 150m (492ft)	Depth: 2m (6½ft) est.

South-south-east of Bowness, Lindeth Lane snakes north to south, linking the B5284 with the A5074. To the east of the lane are several tarns, mostly on private ground. Stonehills Tarn is one of these. There is no public access but it can be seen from the rough track which runs east from the southern end of Lindeth Lane. The tarn has one small island. At its southern end is a dam, over which excess water drains; it is fed by a beck from the north-east. (*About 5 minutes from Lindeth Lane.*)

KNIPE TARN

Grid reference: 427944	Altitude: 146m (480ft)	Depth: 3m (10ft) est.

About 800m (880yds) due east of Stonehills Tarn is the privately owned Knipe Tarn to which there is no public access. The big house overlooks the artificial lake, and at the far end one can see the dam which retains it from the road which passes close by. The excess water flows from the south-eastern end to form the River Gilpin.

ATKINSON TARN

Grid reference: 441947	Altitude: 128m (420ft)	Depth: 2.5m (8ft)

This tarn was created in 1987–8 by the conservation-minded owner of Brow Head Farm, Crook, with advice from a local environmental group and with the aid of a small grant. Triangular in shape, it is supported by an artificial embankment on two sides, has two small islands, and is supplied by a beck flowing from the south-east. Mallard and coot have found a haven here and the

Atkinson Tarn   A recently constructed pond, now stocked with fish.

water has been stocked with fish. The islands have been planted with alder and a mixture of saplings have been encouraged on the rising ground which supports the third, southernmost, side of the triangle.

Although this new tarn is on private ground, it is skirted by a bridleway which connects the B5284 Windermere to Kendal road with Back Lane. (*About 5 minutes along the bridleway from Back Lane.*)

BOLTONS TARN

Grid reference: 448935	Altitude: 187m (614ft)	Depth: 1m (3ft)

Sedge and rush have almost completely obliterated this tarn, leaving only a tiny clear patch of water at its north-eastern corner. Its overgrown condition makes it an attractive site for a multitude of screaming gulls and whirring lapwing. It is accessible from footpaths which extend diagonally (on the Ordnance Survey map) from Crook to Crosthwaite but is scenically unrewarding. (*About 45 minutes from either village.*)

GHYLL HEAD RESERVOIR

Grid reference: 398924	Altitude: 125m (410ft)	Depth: 10m (30ft) est.

South of Bowness the A592 runs alongside Windermere; from it Ghyll Head Road wanders off in a south-easterly direction. Less than 800m (880yds) from the junction, Ghyll Head Reservoir is prominent on the south side of the road. This reservoir holds the domestic water supply for Windermere and district. Set among steep hills draped in the soft greenery of larch and edged by rich meadow grass, it is a delightful stretch of water. Though not a tarn, it is useful as a guide point for other tarns in the vicinity. Trout live in its waters and the fishing is controlled by the Windermere, Ambleside and District Angling Association.

GHYLL HEAD FISH POND (Rosthwaite Tarn)

Grid reference: 397927	Altitude: 128m (420ft)	Depth: 2m (6½ft) est.

On the north side of the road, on private ground opposite Ghyll Head Reservoir, lies Ghyll Head Fish Pond. Held by a dam which sports an ornamental semi-circular stone seat, it can best be seen from the neighbouring National Trust access land to the east. Its alternative name suggests that it may have originally been a smaller natural water.

PODNET (MOSS) TARN (Birkett Houses Tarn)

Grid reference: 405925	Altitude: 130m (426ft)	Depth: 2m (6½ft)

From the entrance to the National Trust access land on Ghyll Head Road and opposite the reservoir of that name a footpath heads north-east towards Winster, across Birkett Houses Allotment. A stone's throw east of this path and concealed beyond two low rock ridges is the intriguing Podnet Tarn, designated a Site of Special Scientific Interest.

At the western end of the tarn, their feet in the water, stand several dead trees. The reason is revealed at the eastern outflow end. Here a low concrete wall with cobbled outflow has been built to raise and stabilise the water level, with the result that the former natural carr development at the opposite end of the tarn has been drowned and terminated.

Hides placed at intervals around the tarn suggest that it may sometimes have been used for shooting. (*About 10–15 minutes from the road.*)

LITTLE LUDDERBURN TARN (Peer How Tarn)

Grid reference: 404916	Altitude: 128m (420ft)	Depth: 2m (6½ft)

At the south end of Ghyll Head Road, near its junction with Birks Road, is a thickly wooded region. To the east of the road a shallow basin lies between Cote Hill and Peer How. Several short becks flow into this marshy area, in the midst of which is the shallow, reed-choked Little Ludderburn Tarn. Birch, alder and willow clothe the margins; bilberry and moss conceal the rocky outcrops, while bogbean, lily and rush press into the water.

A hidden stone stile in the wall bordering the south of the tarn provides access to this no-man's-land – but you are unlikely to escape with dry feet.

CUNSWICK TARN

Grid reference: 489938	Altitude: 136m (446ft)	Depth: 3m (10ft) est.

The limestone escarpment of Cunswick Scar stretches north to south some 2km (1¼miles) west of Kendal, extending southwards as Scout Scar. Prominent footpaths traverse this short-turfed upland; and Cunswick Tarn is clearly visible from the top of the former scar, set in a hollow amid lush meadows and over-shadowed to the east by the steep, wooded escarpment. Through a gate, a steep, slippery track angles down the scarp, levelling into a muddy path which skirts the northern fringe of the tarn.

I watched two coot swim back and forth, beaks in the water, one emitting an explosive 'Phoot!' at intervals. Nearby, a single stag stalked across a meadow, stood a moment, then was gone. The surrounding woodland echoed to the call of the pheasant.

The tarn is a still, deep, muddy water which is supplied by springs from the scarp but appears to have no outlet. (*Allow 40 minutes by footpath from Plumgarth or 1 hour from Kendal.*)

Area I

The next three tarns are located on either side of the Kirkstone Pass which carries the A592, linking the Windermere/Ambleside region in the south with Ullswater and its villages of Patterdale and Glenridding, and ultimately with Penrith in the north. There are two good car parks near the summit and refreshment is close at hand.

SCANDALE TARN (Little Hart Crag Tarn)

Grid reference: 385098	Altitude: 556m (1,825ft)	Depth: 2m (6½ft)

The walk up the Caiston Glen to the head of the Scandale Pass is well worth the effort in itself for the beauty of its cascades and falls, and the impressive water slide of Caiston Beck. The tarn is hidden in a jumble of moraine which descends from Little Hart

Crag to the head of the pass. It is a pleasant but unremarkable pond, said to contain a few trout, though I saw no sign of them below the wind-ruffled surface. Sedge is invading from the eastern fringe, and a tiny stream flows out to the south.

At the head of the pass, follow the track uphill in a northerly direction beside the wall; when the wall bends away you will see the tarn and its satellites. There is convenient parking at the head of Kirkstone Pass, where a clear track leads downhill to the Caiston Beck, crosses by a footbridge, then climbs diagonally left, passing through a fell gate to ascend the true left side of the beck. (*Allow 1–1½ hours from the car park.*)

RED SCREES TARN

Grid reference: 396087	Altitude: 774m (2,540ft)	Depth: 1m (3ft)

This is an example of that rare phenomenon, a summit tarn; set here in a scoop just a few paces from the summit cairn and trig. point where there can be little but direct precipitation to sustain it. It contains no plants. Nearby is another hollow which does not retain water for long after heavy rainfall.

From the summit, the most direct descent to the head of the Kirkstone Pass begins from the cairn and shelter. The initial section is on a sound and exciting path, but lower down overuse has made it perilous in parts. Those prone to vertigo should not attempt it. The best routes are either by way of Scandale Tarn or up the long, gradual ridge from Ambleside, leaving the Kirkstone Road by the track above Roundhill Farm. (*For either route allow 2–2½ hours.*)

CAUDALE HEAD TARN

Grid reference: 414101	Altitude: 745m (2,444ft)	Depth: 1m (3ft)

This peat moss tarn is located on the moorland above the east side of the Kirkstone Pass and just west of Stony Cove Pike. It is easy to find – even in mist – since the path follows the stone wall all the way, ascending from beside the Kirkstone Pass Inn to Raven's Edge above, then northwards towards the tarn. When the path finally curves eastwards towards the summit of Stony Cove Pike, you should see the tarn about 100m (110yds) to the north.

On a bleak January day, shrouded in mist and surrounded by dead moor grass and bare brown peat, it was a lonely place to be. The indented shoreline and residual islands told of the deteriorating peat; in a leeward bay ice held the last vestiges of old snow. Nearby, and to the west, a grey cone topped by a cross transformed itself, as I approached, into the Atkinson Memorial, erected in memory of the late landlords of the Kirkstone Pass Inn – Mark Atkinson who died in 1930 and his son William who passed on in 1987.

As I retraced my steps to the head of the pass, the tops were clearing and sunshine illuminated Red Screes. At the inn I shared a log fire and a pint with the only other occupant – the new landlord. (*Allow 1–1½ hours from the inn.*)

Area J

The Kentmere and Longsleddale Valleys extend northwards towards Harter Fell and the moors south of Haweswater, their upper portions narrowing and their flanks steepening as they penetrate from the Silurian rocks into the Borrowdale Volcanic Group. Above and between the valleys is a series of moorland summits – rocky in the north and rounded towards the south – with saddles of peaty moorland between. Greycrag Tarn and Skeggles Water occupy two of these saddles; the rest, apart from Kentmere Tarn in the valley, are to be found on lower ledges going down towards Staveley and Burneside.

GREYCRAG TARN

Grid reference: 493077	Altitude: 595m (1,953ft)	Depth: 1m (3ft)

Though prominently named on the Ordnance Survey map, I found this a somewhat disappointing tarn. Perhaps all that remains of a former larger tarn, it now consists of four shallow, variously vegetated puddles, located on a broad, marshy saddle between Tarn Crags and Sleddale Fell. The water flows out via the

Galeforth Beck to the River Sprint; the Little Mosedale Beck also drains the saddle and flows east. Stepped grey Borrowdale Volcanic crags overlook the tarn from the north.

Although unrewarding in other ways, Greycrag is the only tarn at this altitude in which I have seen a substantial growth of moorland crowfoot, which was flowering profusely in July. Nearby was a small patch of mares tail and there were several isolated spears of water horsetail in one pond.

A convenient approach is from the car park at the head of Haweswater. Ascend Gatesgarth Pass to the summit, then pick up the eastward track to Mosedale – by contouring across Selside Brow if not too wet – to pick up the line of fence leading to the summit of Tarn Crag. You should see the tarns to the south. (*Allow 1½–2 hours from the car park.*)

KENTMERE TARN

Grid reference: 455030	Altitude: 149m (489ft)	Depth: 9m (29½ft)

The original natural tarn on this site was drained in the 1830s in the hope of improving the agricultural potential of the valley bottom. This proved unsuccessful and the land reverted to rush-covered bog. Then it was discovered that the old tarn bed was rich in diatomite (the silica remains of microscopic freshwater algae called diatoms) which is commercially valuable as a heat insulation material. In the 1930s, three men began to extract the deposit by shovel. Later a dragline was used, and then – as the excavations filled with water – a floating dredger. An aerial ropeway, since removed, transported the material to the nearby works for processing. Although a considerable deposit still remains, it gradually became more economic to import diatomite from abroad, and extraction ceased in 1971.

The present tarn, the result of the excavation, has been stocked with brown and rainbow trout and the fishing is private. During the dredging operations an early fourteenth-century boat of unusual construction was unearthed from the sediment. It is now housed in the National Maritime Museum.

Access is through the works entrance south of the tarn which lies 1km (½ mile) south of Kentmere village and should not be confused with Kentmere Reservoir 5km (3 miles) to the north.

SKEGGLES WATER

Grid reference: 480034	Altitude: 305m (1,000ft)	Depth: 3m (10ft)

The long ridge which extends from north to south between the valleys of Kentmere and Longsleddale broadens into a low saddle halfway along its length. Here, in a hollow amid the glacial debris, nestles Skeggles Water, also – like Kentmere Tarn – said to contain deposits of diatomite. Three small streams flow in from the north-west, while to the south the slow-flowing Skeggles Dyke of deep brown water drains the tarn and is crossed by a wooden footbridge.

In summer this is a particularly attractive tarn, with varied vegetation, much bird life, and pike and perch in its waters; also one has a good chance of being the only visitor.

The long approach via Halls Lane from Staveley offers limited parking; alternatively, there is restricted parking at Kentmere and a shorter approach by tracks from Green Quarter or Long Houses. (*Allow 1–1½ hours from Kentmere.*)

Skeggles Water   Said to contain deposits of diatomite.

TENTER HOWE TARN

Grid reference: 507007	Altitude: 252m (829ft)	Depth: 1m (3ft)

Towards the southern end of Longsleddale, a marshy shoulder juts slightly into the long, deep valley. Here, on this level shoulder, lies Tenter Howe Tarn. It has little open water left, for dense swards of sedge press in on the two remaining open pools. The tarn was once held between two rudimentary stone and earth dams, probably to increase its depth for use as a fish pond in Edwardian times. Now the water fails to reach either dam and the eastern half is overgrown with sphagnum moss.

However within this infilled portion is a large stone tank containing clear water about 2m (6½ft) in depth, probably spring fed. The tarn itself is maintained by a spring or natural seepage, and has some fine views to the north.

Though unnamed on the map, the tarn may be approached by paths through Nether House Farm, Tenter Howe Farm or Bridge End Farm. There is limited roadside parking just south of Dale End where a footpath crosses the River Sprint and joins the path leading to the farms and the tarn. (*Allow 30–40 minutes from Dale End.*)

KEMP TARN

Grid reference: 464988	Altitude: 218m (715ft)	Depth: 1m (3ft) est.

North of the steep Reston Scar, which overlooks the village of Staveley, is an undulating plateau with many hollows containing small ponds. The largest of these is Kemp Tarn, a shallow water supporting a wide variety of aquatic plants.

Although the tarn is on private agricultural land, the farmer is not averse to well-behaved parties inspecting it. Two footpaths from Brow Lane, Staveley, and one from beside Bailey Bridge over the River Kent, converge above the village to provide access to the tarn which lies just beyond the fell gate. (*About 30 minutes using any of the footpaths.*)

Tarns on Potter Fell

At the southern extremity of the high land situated between the Kentmere and Longsleddale valleys, Potter Fell boasts eight tarns, all privately owned by the Cropper family who also control the paper mill at Burneside. (Several of the tarns have been dammed and enlarged to provide water for the paper mill.) Those tarns which are accessible to the public can be reached by footpaths from the Potter Fell Road which follows the National Park boundary north of Burneside.

GURNAL DUBS (Fothergill Tarn)

Grid reference: 503992	Altitude: 286m (938ft)	Depth: 4.5m (15ft)

What a delightful water this is, especially when a clear sky and bright sunshine dress it in blue and silver. A notice informs us that the fishing is controlled by the Kent Angling Association – and very good fishing it is, according to the angler I met there.

Originally three small ponds or 'dubs', the tarn has been formed into one large water by a dam; the indigenous wild brown trout have been augmented by fresh stock. The unobtrusive dam is clad in stone and turf; a stone-built boathouse on the western shore,

Gurnal Dubs   A stone boathouse stands beside this trout fishery, which also supplies water for the Burneside paper mill.

originally erected by the Fothergill family, is in an excellent state of repair. The single tree-clad island adds an air of maturity to this beautiful tarn.

A footpath crosses the dam and continues westwards towards Potter Tarn. The nearest point of access from the Potter Fell Road is by the footpath north of Larchbank Farm to the fell track at Birk Rigg. This enables one to visit all the tarns in this area which are accessible to the public. (*Allow 40–50 minutes from the road.*)

POTTER TARN

Grid reference: 494989	Altitude: 245m (804ft)	Depth: 6m (19½ft) est.

On a visit in 1989 the drained remains of Potter Tarn languished within a brown saucer of dried mud and water-washed pebbles. Exposed stone walls, drowned when the dam was full, reached down to the water's edge.

A more recent visit in 1991 confirmed my suspicion that the water had been drained because the concrete dam wall had deteriorated. A brand new spillway had been constructed, lowering the volume of water to a level that could be safely contained by the old dam walls.

The footpath from Gurnal Dubs crosses the spillway below the dam wall and continues to Staveley; another follows the outflow towards Ghyll Pool. En route to Ghyll Pool are the remains of a small fish pond with stone channelled inflow and outflow, complete with stone fishing platforms, all ruined now. The water is almost entirely choked with sedge, bogbean, cotton grass and rush. (*Potter Tarn is about 15 minutes from Gurnal Dubs.*)

GHYLL POOL

Grid reference: 497984	Altitude: 220m (722ft)	Depth: 4m (12ft) est.

The outflow from Potter Tarn flows south for some 450m (490yds) before entering Ghyll Pool, a reservoir held by another concrete dam built in 1934. A notice tells us that it is the property of James Cropper & Co Ltd, to be used for drinking water only. Fishing, swimming and boating are forbidden. The track continues south to the Potter Fell Road.

To the east of Gurnal Dubs lie the Taggleshaw and Routen Beck tarns; all are on private ground and there is no public right of access. The three Taggleshaws form a semi-circle round Gurnal Dubs.

LOW TAGGLESHAW

Grid reference: 505989	Altitude: 288m (945ft)	Depth: 1m (3ft) est.

Beside the fell track which approaches Gurnal Dubs from the south is this much overgrown tarn, choked with bogbean, sedge, rush and cotton grass. Very little clear water remains; with the larger tarn only 180m (196yds) away, there is little here to merit attention.

MIDDLE TAGGLESHAW

Grid reference: 507993	Altitude: 297m (974ft)	Depth: 1m (3ft) est.

Again, vegetation has obliterated most of the water surface of this tarn. It lies amid a scooped, hollowed and grooved landscape much favoured by black-headed gulls and lapwings.

HIGH TAGGLESHAW

Grid reference: 505994	Altitude: 308m (1,011ft)	Depth: 0.5m (1½ft)

Unlike its sisters, this tarn has not yet succumbed completely to invasion by sedge. Although it is only a shallow pond with a single island, it offers sanctuary to black-headed gulls.

UPPER ROUTEN BECK TARN

Grid reference: 511992	Altitude: 257m (843ft)	Depth: 1m (3ft)

To the east of the Taggleshaw Tarns, Routen Beck flows south-east to join the River Sprint, swelling in two places to form the Upper and Lower Routen Beck Tarns.

A rock-cored moraine extends across the valley, blocking the path of the beck to create the upper tarn. The outflow has cut a narrow V-shaped channel on the true right of the valley to pass the obstruction. In contrast to the Taggleshaws, this tarn has clear, open water, a mud bottom and a rush-trimmed perimeter; it also sustains a growth of water starwort and stonewort.

LOWER ROUTEN BECK TARN

Grid reference: 514991	Altitude: 245m (804ft)	Depth: 1.5m (5ft) est.

A pretty tarn, irregular in shape, Lower Routen Beck is dotted with several small islands and favoured by black-headed gulls and oystercatchers. The south shore is gravel, gently sloping to a rocky bottom; the rest of the shoreline is steep, while the perimeter is firm and mainly grass-edged.

Area K

Although the tarns in this final section lie outside the National Park they have been included because among them are three interesting examples of waters with dense willow carr. They are to be found north of Kendal and east of the A6 trunk road, where rocks of the Silurian and Carboniferous series intermingle, both heavily overlaid with glacial deposits.

SKELSMERGH TARN

Grid reference: 534967	Altitude: 107m (350ft)	Depth: 5m (16½ft)

Before I approached this sinister tarn, local enquiries revealed that it had whirlpools and was known to be bottomless. These comments were too intriguing to ignore. Several visits, latterly with a rubber dinghy and a considerable length of plumbline, elicited the facts but sadly destroyed the myths.

The whirlpools are probably caused by swirling winds, often seen on lakes and tarns in stormy conditions. Furthermore, the term 'bottomless' refers not to its depth but to the fact that there is no firm bottom, only soft mud which makes the tarn extremely dangerous.

Skelsmergh receives its water mainly from springs and the seepage of groundwater; there is an outflow to the south by way of a dug channel – apparently a former attempt to drain the tarn. The water is alkaline, due to the presence of limestone nearby.

Skelsmergh Tarn   This mysterious 'bottomless' tarn has a sinister atmosphere, despite its fringe of delightful lilies.

This pond is of the lowland type surrounded by dense willow carr; along with several others in the area, it may occupy a former 'kettle hole' (a depression caused by residual blocks of ice becoming detached from declining glaciers). The water is edged with bogbean, club rush and white water lily and contains roach and rudd.

The tarn, designated a Site of Special Scientific Interest, lies just off the Dales Way, from which a footpath, unclear on the ground, extends northwards. Halfway between Skelsmergh Tarn and the village of Otter Bank is another area of dense carr with small residual ponds, perhaps the remnant of a former tarn.

From a layby on the A6 at 529965, the single track road east leads to Tarn Bank, where there is a short path going northwards to the tarn. (*Allow 20 minutes from the layby*.)

BLACK MOSS TARN

Grid reference: 548971	Altitude: 176m (577ft)	Depth: 2m (6½ft)

Just south of Patton Bridge which leaps the River Mint, a waymarked track, the Dales Way, crosses the road; its westward extension passes through Bigland Farm and in less than 500m (550yds) skirts Black Moss Tarn. (Skelsmergh Tarn, see above, is 1.6km (1 mile) further west along the path.)

Black Moss Tarn is situated at the head of a shallow valley among high, walled pasture land. It is triangular in shape, with a grassy, treeless shoreline; on the main island grows an alder sapling, the other three islets are rush-covered. Water horsetail is present at the eastern end and bogbean at the marshy western end but the most prominent marginal plant is yellow flag iris.

Fish were rising at the time of my visit, though I believe the tarn only contains privately fished pike and perch. I also saw coot and mallard. A deep, dug channel drains the water towards the north but there is no surface inflow. (*Allow 30 minutes from Patton Bridge.*)

WHINFELL TARN

Grid reference: 559980	Altitude: 138m (452ft)	Depth: 3m (10ft) est.

Whinfell is a large, open tarn with few trees and surrounded by low morainic hills of lush, walled pastures which slope gently down to the water's edge. Springs to the north maintain this lovely tarn, while the outflow southwards finds the River Mint. The water holds perch, rudd, roach, tench, pike and eels. However the marshy western bay is used as a rubbish tip and farm vehicles are parked indiscriminately on the shore nearby. Farm roads and paths surround the tarn. (*About 10–15 minutes from Patton Bridge.*)

FLAT TARN

Grid reference: 564987	Altitude: 155m (508ft)	Depth: 2m (7ft) est.

From Greyrigg village on the A685 a minor road runs north, then north-west, and after 2km (1¼ miles), passes Flat Farm. Behind the farm to the east, amid lush pasture land, is a shallow depression occupied by a small, circular, carr-fringed tarn to which there is no public access. Invasive beds of common reed and mats of water lilies press concentrically in on the remaining open water. There appears to be no surface inflow and it greatly resembles a miniature Skelsmergh Tarn or nearby Peggy Tarn.

PEGGY TARN

Grid reference: 569976	Altitude: 136m (446ft)	Depth: 2.5m (8ft) est.

Access to the vicinity of Peggy Tarn, which is set in agricultural land, is by way of indistinct public footpaths from either the A685 west of Greyrigg or from the minor road which runs northwards and westwards from the village. Your best bet is to make for Tarnside House (derelict at the time of my visit), which is near the tarn.

This oval water is almost a replica of Flat Tarn in size, situation and condition, common reed and water lilies leaving only a small area of open water at the eastern end. In fact the carr and reed fen are so dense that the tarn is virtually inaccessible. The bedrock in the area appears to be carboniferous limestone, covered here by thick moraine deposits, resulting in a landscape of rich, undulating pasture land.

GRAYRIGG TARN

Grid reference: 596981	Altitude: 224m (735ft)	Depth: 2.5m (8ft)

Grayrigg tarn is situated beside the A685 Kendal to Tebay road, about 1km (½ mile) east of the village of Greyrigg. Like many of the tarns in this eastern region of Cumbria, it occupies a near-circular depression in an area full of glacial deposits. The surrounding land is bordering on moorland pasture and the tarn receives its water supply from surface drainage, mainly from the northern fellsides. The strong north-westerly outflow turns abruptly south-west and joins other drainage channels to form the Grayrigg Hall Beck. The water has been stocked with rainbow trout by the owners for private fishing. Bordering the eastern shore is a narrow belt of willow carr; the rest of the tarn is open, apart from an edging of common reed, club rush, water horsetail, water lily and bogbean.

The Tarns
of South-West
Lakeland

The south-west region of Lakeland, as defined by the
Ordnance Survey Outdoor Leisure 6 map, contains 53
named tarns or groups of tarns within the National Park
boundary, here blocked into areas labelled 'A' to 'I' on the
key map. The region encompasses the high central fells from
Gable and the Scafells, Bowfell and the head of Langdale, to
Coniston Old Man and his companions. The Great Langdale and Coniston valleys thrust deeply from the east and
south and the wild western dales of Wasdale, Eskdale and
Dunnerdale penetrate from the Solway coast. South-West
Lakeland contains some of the finest walking for the tarn-
hunter – and some of the highest tarns, to be sought only by
the experienced and fully equipped fell-walker.

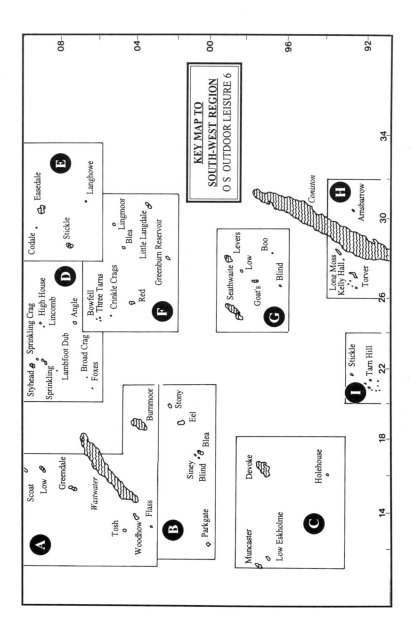

KEY MAP TO
SOUTH-WEST REGION
O S OUTDOOR LEISURE 6

Area A

Wasdale has seven tarns, suited to walkers of differing abilities. The first three are on the low land just west of Wastwater; the remaining four are high tarns requiring committed walking in the fells which flank the lake.

TOSH TARN

Grid reference: 128053	Altitude: 88m (288ft)	Depth: 2.5m (8ft)

Just south of the higher Gosforth to Wasdale Head road, a rough lane leads to the farmstead of Gill; the tarn lies across the fields to the west. This is agricultural land and there is no public access without permission; anglers are not welcome.

In 1976, and again in 1989, the tarn dried out into two ponds separated by a ridge of gravel on which a stone cairn had been built. When I visited I was told that 'Jimmy Crane' (the heron) had gone with the trout but by late summer of '89 the tarn level had been restored, the cairn was barely visible and rising fish showed that some of their number had survived the blue-grey predator.

The nature of the surrounding ground suggests that the tarn occupies a depression where lateral moraine was previously deposited close to the northern flank of the valley. The inflow is by way of a small stream from the north; where the exit stream emerges, there is a deep V-cut channel which may once have been the outflow for a larger water body.

The tarn bottom consists of stones and gravel and the water is edged with oaks, hawthorn and hazel.

WOODHOW TARN

Grid reference: 136043	Altitude: 65m (213ft)	Depth: 2m (6½ft)

About 1km (½ mile) east of Nether Wasdale along the road towards Wastwater, is Woodhow Farm. From here a signed footpath leads north-westwards, beside the eastern shore of the tarn. In contrast to Tosh Tarn, Woodhow occupies a slight depression in the centre of the Wasdale Valley where level

Woodhow Tarn   Wastwater and its screes lie just behind the ridge.

meadows extend towards the River Irt, the outflow from Wastwater. Its stony bottom and low banks of crumbly glacial debris suggest that it is probably the remnant of a much larger late glacial lake.

A small stream enters from the north-east but the intermittent south-westerly outflow means that the water is virtually stagnant. Trees dot the northern shore; otherwise it has an open aspect. Water lilies occur in scattered clumps and I noticed some moorhens. Pike and perch are said to inhabit the water. (*From the roadside allow 10 minutes, though lack of parking may necessitate a longer trek.*) Alternatively, park at the triangle just north of Forest Bridge (129038), from where circular walks to the tarn may be devised, using the Ordnance Survey map.

FLASS TARN

Grid reference: 129035	Altitude: 60m (196ft)	Depth: 45cm (1½ft)

Just south of the River Irt, near Forest Bridge at Nether Wasdale, a signed footpath beside Flass House leads south-eastwards across fields to a plantation of Scots pines. At the edge of the trees lies Flass Tarn.

In summer it is barely distinguishable from the surrounding grassland, being almost completely overgrown by a surprisingly wide variety of aquatic plants for so small a pond. It is held by a low, raised bank, suggesting that it was once a small artificial fish pond. An intermittent stream supplies water from the south and the outflow is to the north-west; neither of these runners was flowing at the time of my August visit.

About 75m (80yds) to the west is another small pond overshadowed by a pair of Scots pines. (*About 10 minutes from the road.*)

GREENDALE TARN

Grid reference: 147075	Altitude: 402m (1,320ft)	Depth: 9m (29½ft)

From the Gosforth to Wasdale road, the effort of the steep ascent beside Greendale Gill is amply repaid by the beauty of the heather-clad fellside across the beck and the falls of Tongues Gills which flow in from Buckbarrow Moss. All the way one has the rushing water for company. The track levels out on to gently sloping moorland dotted with an ample scattering of rocks, perhaps a mixture of moraine from the glacier which scooped the Greendale Tarn hollow, and a later accumulation of avalanche debris from the crags of Middle Fell.

The smooth outline of this long, narrow tarn is enlivened by the conglomeration of huge boulders poised on the steep eastern fellside. Opposite, on the western shore, the marshy ground rises less steeply and is dotted with many curious mounds of raised sphagnum moss. Two main becks contribute to the tarn, one from the west and one from the north. It is likely that brown trout are present. (*Allow 1 hour from the road.*)

SCOAT TARN

Grid reference: 159104	Altitude: 596m (1,956ft)	Depth: 20m (65½ft)

The rising track from Nether Bridge beside Wastwater leads steadily upwards, alongside the west bank of Nether Beck, where the rushing water from the tarn passes through two deep gorges overhung with dark-leaved holly and 'bead-bonny ash' (as Gerard Manley Hopkins described the rowan in his poem 'Inversnaid'). In brilliant autumn sunshine this is God's own country. Nether Beck curves in from the right and leads on to the steep, bouldery moraine which holds the tarn.

Tarns, when approached from below, tend to keep their presence a secret until the last moment; Scoat Tarn is no exception. The flat-topped moraine retains the water almost at its own height so that one cannot at first distinguish between level mountain grass and level water.

Two energetic becks flow in from the north from the slopes of Scoat Fell, and round the tarn to the south-east hummocky mounds of moraine cast curved shadows in the lowering sun. These high Wasdale tarns share one feature – they all face south-west.

Fine, but small, trout are said to inhabit the water. (*About 1½–2 hours from Nether Bridge.*)

LOW TARN

Grid reference: 162093	Altitude: 519m (1,704ft)	Depth: 3m (10ft)

From Scoat Tarn, a southerly course over a gentle ridge will bring one to within sight of Low Tarn, and on a clear day what a view unfolds! The tarn lies at one's feet; beyond, the craggy ridge of Yewbarrow dips down towards Wastwater and beyond that again, the whole Scafell range – from Great End to Scafell itself – stands out in profile.

When I visited the tarn, its waters lay placid and clear; green and gold grasses framed its shallow fringes and fish rings expanded lazily on its surface, while wet boulders gleamed along its margin. Secret streams murmured and slipped, still chuckling, into the tarn.

This lovely water occupies a very shallow south-west facing combe, which might more accurately be described as a shelf.

The return beside Brimfull Beck leads to a prominent track beside Over Beck and eventually to the car park at Overbeck Bridge beside Wastwater. (*From Scoat Tarn, allow about 20–30 minutes.*)

Low Tarn Beyond the ridge of Yewbarrow stand the Scafells and linking Mickledore.

BURNMOOR TARN

Grid reference: 184044	Altitude: 253m (830ft)	Depth: 13m (42½ft)

This is said to be the third-largest tarn in Lakeland. (Devoke Water is the largest, followed by Seathwaite Tarn.) Burnmoor Tarn stands at the head of Miterdale, flanked by huge moraines, on the broad ridge that separates Wasdale and Eskdale. Miterdale would have been its natural outfall, had not a low moraine been deposited in its path. (This obstacle can be clearly seen at the far end of the tarn when viewed from Bulatt Bridge where the outflow now escapes by way of Whillan Beck to Eskdale.)

The tarn is impressive but not beautiful; the grim Burnmoor Lodge with its twisted tree, once a keeper's cottage, stands sentinel over the windswept water and the bare moorland. A plaque inscribed with a religious text is plastered on to the gable end; and

75

a wooden dispenser, empty at my passing, was apparently intended to proffer comforting tracts to the wayward traveller.

In early August, a 2m (6½ft) belt of water lobelia girded the shallow eastern shore, pale violet heads on slender stalks nodding rhythmically, trumpets at the dip and facing uniformly away from the breeze. Otherwise, there is little surface vegetation; far out the bed falls to over 13m (42½ft) and brown trout, pike and perch can be fished for.

The tarn can be reached by paths from Miterdale and Eskdale but perhaps the most convenient – and shortest – approach is from the National Trust car park at Wasdale Head where a well-marked track, once used by funeral cortèges heading for the church at Boot in Eskdale, passes the tarn. (*Allow 1–1½ hours from Wasdale Head.*)

Area B

The lakeless Eskdale valley is the centre for this group; apart from Parkgate and Eskdale Green tarns, all but Low Birker Tarn occur on the dividing ridge between the Eskdale and Wasdale valleys. Low Birker is the only named tarn on the south side.

PARKGATE TARN (Santon Bridge Tarn)

Grid reference: 118006	Altitude: 68m (223ft)	Depth: 2m (6½ft)

Less than 400m (440yds) along the road east of Santon Bridge a bridle path on the right is signposted to Slapestones. Follow this in a southerly direction for 1km (½ mile), to where another track from Parkgate joins from the right. There is a wooden guide post here, and the tarn is only a few steps away.

This modest water, once a smaller natural tarn enlarged to form an ornamental lake and fish pond for the park at Irton Hall, is sadly beginning to lose much of its former glory. It contains some of the finest beds of water lilies I have seen in this region but, due to the declining water level, those inshore are high and nearly dry.

A low dam encloses the water along the south-west fringe but it is so overgrown that it is difficult to approach. Here, a nick in the barrier releases a steady overflow which may be the cause of the tarn's demise.

The skeleton of the former boathouse still stands on the north-west margin but sphagnum moss has invaded the shoreline to such an extent that its inlet is completely overgrown. The promontory extending from the north-east is dotted with rhododendrons and many of the original surrounding oak, ash, holly and birch trees remain, but the whole is now being engulfed by coniferous forest. (*From the road allow 40 minutes.*)

ESKDALE GREEN TARN (Gatehouse Tarn)

Grid reference: 145001	Altitude: 37m (121ft)	Depth: 4m (13ft) est.

This circular ornamental pond created in Victorian times stands in the private grounds of the Gate House, now occupied by the famous Outward Bound Mountain School. It has a wide range of aquatic plants, including white water lily.

BLEA TARN, ESKDALE

Grid reference: 165010	Altitude: 218m (715ft)	Depth: 5m (16½ft) est.

The famous miniature steam passenger railway, La'al Ratty, begins its journey at Ravenglass and runs along the Eskdale Valley, sounding its evocative steam whistle as it nears the terminus at Dalegarth Station. Directly above Beckfoot Station (the one before the terminus), a signed path leads to a group of three tarns, of which Blea is the largest, and well worth the steep climb. A less steep approach begins from a lane just east of the Eskdale Outward Bound School, passing across the Ratty line to Hollin How, and on by a green lane to the tarn. Yet another possible route begins at Eskdale Green and runs beside the northern boundary of the school.

A shallow south-west-facing combe holds Blea Tarn, a pleasant water, from which there are extensive views of the lower Eskdale Fells and beyond to the Irish Sea. The setting is a broad, ice-smoothed ridge of rocky knolls between Eskdale and Miterdale. On a sunny August day, when I visited, the sparkling water was

Blea Tarn (Eskdale)   This rock-edged channel leads the tarn outflow to its final plunge towards Eskdale.

stirred by a gentle breeze and lapped at the rocky shore where water lobelia raised their blooms above the surface.

There is no surface inflow but a strong stream emerges from the south-western end to pass through a tiny pond before descending steeply to join the River Esk below. (*Allow 1½–2 hours from Eskdale Green or 30 minutes from Beckfoot Station.*)

SINEY TARN

Grid reference: 163012	Altitude: 224m (735ft)	Depth: 50cm (1½ft)

Near Blea Tarn, Siney sits on glacial debris in a broad, shallow saucer between ice-smoothed, partly grassed mounds of grey rock. The open water is being invaded from the shore inwards and from the island of sedge outwards, and the surrounding area oozes water as one walks. A black-headed gull wheeled protectively above two fluffy brown chicks who seemed unconcerned by my presence. (*To reach Siney Tarn, take the path north-west from the Blea Tarn outflow – about 3–5 minutes walk.*)

BLIND TARN, ESKDALE

Grid reference: 163010	Altitude: 225m (738ft)	Depth: 1m (3ft)

Just south of Siney a small elongated pond survives, despite the rushes which encroach upon it. The name 'Blind' probably refers to the fact that there is no surface inflow or outflow; all water movement occurs below the spongy surface. The area of marshland within which these two tarns lie is said to be subject to will-o'-the-wisp phenomena, also present around nearby Eel Tarn. These flickering lights seen in marshy areas are caused by the spontaneous combustion of marsh gas – possibly methane. (*About 5 minutes from Blea Tarn, just to the left of the path between this and Siney Tarn.*)

EEL TARN

Grid reference: 189019	Altitude: 198m (650ft)	Depth: 2m (6½ft)

This natural tarn is sunk in the glacial drift of a shallow marshy basin, where the surrounding bog makes it difficult to approach the eastern shore. To the north-east, smoothed rock tors rise in

Eel Tarn   North beyond the distant col lies Yewbarrow, with Pillar and Haycock beyond.

tiers to the rugged horizon, beyond which lies Stony Tarn. Eel
Tarn contrasts with its near neighbour in its shallowness, more
open aspect and soft bed. The plants, too, vary. Here, small white
water lilies form the principal vegetation, while club rush and
sedge grace the southern edge.

A signposted track begins from the valley road at 186009 and
another from behind the Woolpack Inn; either may be followed
easily to the tarn. There is limited parking on the verge opposite
Wha House Farm, 1km (½ mile) east of the Woolpack. (*From
here, allow 45 minutes to the tarn.*)

STONY TARN

Grid reference: 199025	Altitude: 300m (985ft)	Depth: 5m (16ft)

Surrounded on three sides by high ground, which descends in a
series of rocky outcrops, is this secluded water. A noisy beck
enters from the north, while the outflow follows a flat-bottomed,
drift-filled valley away to the south, soon to lose its way among
the grey tors. At its emergence from the tarn, the outflow crosses a
rib of smooth bolster-like rock which extends some distance on
either side to merge with the surrounding crags. Could this be a
true rock basin?

The condition of the tarn floor, covered with sharp-edged blocks
of stone, justifies its name; in summer, sedge and water lobelia grace
the northern and southern shores and dragonflies abound.

If visiting Eel Tarn first, the best approach is from the southern
end of that water. The path, where it exists, is little more than a
faint sheep trod but one should aim for a distant, pointed rock
pinnacle which reveals itself occasionally. Maintain a north-
easterly course through easier ground until the outflow from
Stony Tarn is reached. An alternative route begins from behind
the Woolpack Inn, as indicated by the pecked black line on the
Ordnance Survey map, and bears right (instead of left for Eel
Tarn), passing Peelplace Naddle to follow the outflow to Stony
Tarn.

The reverse of this latter route will return one to the road at Wha
House Farm. Instead of returning to the Woolpack, follow Blea
Beck in a south-westerly direction. Then, when it curves away
south-east, continue on the original line to parallel the wall that

Stony Tarn In the foreground a noisy beck rushes to fill this seldom-visited tarn.

skirts Hare Crag and pick up the Scafell track that leads downhill to the road. (*From Eel Tarn allow 30 minutes; 45 minutes from the Woolpack Inn via Peelplace Naddle.*)

LOW BIRKER TARN

Grid reference: 191995	Altitude: 248m (814ft)	Depth: 2m (6½ft)

This tarn lies in the north-west corner of Birker Moor, a flat marshy area situated on a shelf above and to the south of Eskdale Valley. The beck which drains the moor – and the tarn – flows north and descends steeply, as Birker Force, to join the River Esk.

From the convenient roadside parking space opposite Wha House Farm at 201009, a pleasant route begins from Wha House Bridge, follows the Esk south, then west through Penny Hill Farm to Doctor Bridge. Do not cross the bridge, but go south to

Low Birker Farm. Here the left-hand fork behind the farm follows the old peat road which zigzags up the fellside as a broad green track, past a roofless stone building. Where the climb levels off, take the left-hand fork – there is a small cairn in amongst the bracken – and follow the track which skirts the high ground towards Tarn Crag. (On the OS map the track is shown by a faint black pecked line; the more prominent green pecked line indicates only the general trend of the right of way but does not refer to the route on the ground.)

The tear-shaped tarn, held to the west by a low moraine, reveals itself below Tarn Crag. This charming pond, sparkling in the sunlight when I arrived, soon took on a more sombre mood as cloud moved in from the south. Heather moor reaches to the edge of the tarn except where spaghnum moss curls a lime-green lip. Bur-reed, water lobelia and the ubiquitous bogbean grow here.

Returning to Doctor Bridge and on to the nearby Woolpack Inn for refreshment rounds off the excursion very pleasantly. If energy permits, the walk may be completed by taking in Eel and Stony Tarns. (*Allow 1½ hours from Wha House Farm to Low Birker Tarn.*)

Area C

South of Eskdale, a whaleback of high moorland extends southwards to Black Combe, a southern outcropping of the Skiddaw Slates. This moorland separates the Duddon Valley from the coastal plain south of Ravenglass. Devoke Water and Holehouse Tarn are situated at its northern end; on the coastal plain, at about the same latitude as Black Combe, is Barfield Tarn. Unfortunately this tarn is too far south to be included on the Outdoor Leisure 6 Ordnance Survey map; you will therefore need to refer to the Landranger 96 map. Muncaster Tarn is to be found on the fascinating little ridge of Muncaster Fell just inland from Ravenglass and separated from the moorland to the south by the River Esk.

DEVOKE WATER

Grid reference: 158969	Altitude: 235m (770ft)	Depth: 14m (46ft)

The approach, from the Eskdale to Ulpha road by way of a bridle track, leads to the western end of this, the largest Lakeland tarn. The surrounding grim moorland and the waves lapping the rock-strewn, marshy shore create a sense of desolation which is intensified by the bleak two-storey boathouse-cum-refuge and its ruined stable. Far more interesting, in my view, is the more sheltered western end where a broad moraine blocks what must once have been a valley.

The blocked-off valley is occupied by a small stream, Black Beck; the main outflow exits to the north-west through a low point of the moraine, flowing gently for a short distance, before plunging over a rock lip, down an 8m (26ft) cascade and away through a deep V-cut ravine towards the River Esk. Extensive moraines flank the tarn, with crags protruding here and there, the whole possessing something of the character of Burnmoor Tarn. The only prominent emergent plant, apart from the ubiquitous rush, is water lobelia, which adorns the shallow margins in the summer.

The tarn is part of the Muncaster Estate and the fishing is controlled by the Millom Angling Association. (*Allow 15–20 minutes from the road.*)

HOLEHOUSE TARN

Grid reference: 155940	Altitude: 172m (564ft)	Depth: 1m (3ft)

A ring of laughing blue water appeared one April morning as I came over the broad ridge which extends southwards from Devoke Water to Black Combe. Although Holehouse is a peat moss tarn of little merit in itself, sunk among peat hags and dried grasses, it has a superb panorama of mountain scenery as its north-eastern backdrop. The lonely, trackless wasteland it occupies rang, at intervals, to the trill of the rising lark; while a brisk, cool easterly wind darkened the water surface, sending endless ripples to expire silently along the western margin. Around the lee shore, cases discarded by caddis fly larvae littered the rocky bottom; in one favoured inlet dozens of jewel-like whirligig beetles spun on the surface, attended by several water boatmen rowing jerkily back and forth. One would not have expected to see so much life on this barren moor.

This tarn is the source of Holehouse Beck, a tributary of the Duddon. On the ridge between the tarn and Devoke Water is much evidence of the presence of early man; disused copper mines from more recent times can be found below Hesk Fell.

A convenient approach to the tarn is from Millbrow. Go through the farm at Bigert Mire and take the grass track westward, skirting north of Whitfield, then contouring north towards the craggy summit of Stainton Pike. (*About 1 hour.*)

MUNCASTER TARN (Chapel Hill Tarn)

Grid reference: 106978	Altitude: 152m (498ft)	Depth: 5m (16½ft) est.

About 500m (550yds) east of the car park and entrance to Muncaster Castle is Fell Lane, a public bridleway that goes along the spine of Muncaster Fell to form two branches which eventually arrive at Eskdale Green near two of the La'al Ratty railway stations. You can take the famous steam train back to Ravenglass, then take either of the two footpaths from the southern end of the village to get back almost to the car park. This, together with a visit to the castle, would make an excellent day's outing.

But what of the tarn, you ask. Oh, it lies about 1km (½ mile) along Fell Lane near the start of the walk, on the left-hand side of the path, but is almost completely obscured from view by dense beds of rhododendrons.

Bogbean, yellow water lily and the common reed are the main plant residents. This tarn is man-made and was probably once used for fishing. (*About 35 minutes from the car park.*)

LOW ESKHOLME TARN

Grid reference: 113973	Altitude: 9m (30ft)	Depth: 2m (6½ft) est.

Visiting this tarn in winter was not a good idea, and it would probably have been no better in summer. It was surrounded by wetland and so completely engulfed by scrub and aquatic growth that no clear water could be seen. Not recommended.

BARFIELD TARN

Grid reference: 107869	Altitude: 24m (79ft)	Depth: 4m (13ft) est.

Black Combe abruptly rears its 600m (1,968ft) head just north of Millom, at the south-western edge of the National Park. It receives the full force of the south-westerly rain-bearing winds from across the Irish Sea, and much of the rainfall drains down steep becks which have cut deeply into its western flank. (The run-off gathers on the narrow coastal plain to form the River Annas.)

One of these becks pauses in a dip among the low coastal hills to form Barfield Tarn, a pond of enriched water hosting a wide variety of aquatics. Most noticeable are beds of the common reed that almost encircle the pond and have developed on the north-eastern shore from reed fen into dense but stunted willow carr.

The tarn lies on agricultural pasture land to which there is no access without permission. However an excellent view can be had from the lane that leads to Barfield from the A595. It's possible to park beside the A595 about 500m (550yds) north of the lane. (*Allow 20 minutes to walk to the viewpoint.*)

Area D

Here are the highest tarns which lie between the head of Borrowdale and the Scafells. All are located on Borrowdale Volcanic Group rocks which produce the magnificent, rugged scenery of the high central fells. These tarns should only be visited by experienced and properly equipped walkers.

STYHEAD TARN

Grid reference: 222098	Altitude: 436m (1,430ft)	Depth: 8.5m (29ft)

Perhaps surprisingly for a tarn set about by great fells, Styhead is in my opinion exceedingly dull. It has a plain shoreline with marshy deltas, the surrounding slopes of Green Gable, Great

Styhead Tarn   The familiar view towards Borrowdale seen by the thousands who walk this route over Sty Head Pass.

Gable and Seathwaite Fell being somewhat featureless. Skiddaw may be glimpsed in the distance.

As well as occupying a scooped hollow in glacial deposits, Styhead Tarn has been dammed by downwashed bouldery scree from Aaron Slack. It is well supplied with water from the slopes of Gable, Styhead Pass and the outflow from Sprinkling Tarn, and is reputed to contain small brown trout.

Every summer many thousands of walkers pass this tarn en route from Stockley Bridge to climb the neighbouring fells and campers sometimes find a resting place on its grassy green shores. To reach the tarn, follow the broad track south from Seathwaite Farm to Stockley Bridge. Cross the bridge, pass through the gate and continue in a westerly direction up the steep, repaired path to reach the tarn. (*Allow 1 hour from Seathwaite.*)

SPRINKLING TARN

Grid reference: 228092	Altitude: 597m (1,960ft)	Depth: 9m (29½ft)

Beneath the gullied crag of Great End, this delightful tarn occupies a gouged hollow amidst humped moraine on the upper reaches of Seathwaite Fell. Lying beside the busy track which runs from Styhead to Esk Hause, its many bays and promontories and its fine view of Gable make this a water well worth visiting, especially on a sunny summer day when a cooling swim can be enjoyed near its shallow fringes. The water drains to the north-west and descends some 150m (500ft) to Styhead Tarn. Small brown trout survive here. (*About 45 minutes walk from Styhead.*)

SPRINKLING CRAG TARN (Great Slack Tarn)

Grid reference: 228095	Altitude: 617m (2,025ft)	Depth: 1.5m (5ft)

Some 200m (220yds) due north of Sprinkling Tarn lies this small water, the largest of several ponds scattered on the upper portion of Seathwaite Fell. Shaped like a teardrop and backed by a small crag, it is seldom visited. Water seeps in from the surrounding moraine and water lobelia and broadleaved pondweed may be found here.

ANGLE TARN, LANGDALE

Grid reference: 244076	Altitude: 565m (1,854ft)	Depth: 15m (49ft)

This fine corrie tarn is held in a scooped bowl at the foot of the crags of Hanging Knott. It is amply supplied by small becks from the encircling crags and moraine, while the outflowing Angletarn Gill spills over a rocky lip to join Langstrath Beck. Trout are said to be plentiful but small, due to the lack of sustenance in its green depths.

Colin Dodgson once described to me how he and Timothy Tyson, his companion of many tarn swims, had come upon the frozen tarn one winter and built a cairn in the middle of the ice, one curling the stones out from the shore while the other constructed the pile – a somewhat risky venture! (*Allow 40 minutes south-east from Sprinkling Tarn via Esk Hause.*)

LAMBFOOT DUBB

Grid reference: 221084	Altitude: 682m (2,240ft)	Depth: 1m (3ft)

High above the Corridor Route from Styhead to Scafell Pike, this striking little pool or 'dub' perches audaciously on the very summit of a ridge, protected from extinction by only a metre of mossy peat and rubble at either end. From this wonderfully clear jewel of a tarn one may gaze northwards towards the bulk of Gable, or south to the ridge with its well-worn track and endless procession of silhouettes moving to and fro from Scafell Pikes. Here, in late April, swam water boatmen and whirligig beetles and, most surprisingly, I saw a small clutch of frog spawn beside the water.

Lambfoot Dubb   This tiny tarn is perched on a narrow col above the Corridor Route. Great Gable and Kirkfell lie behind.

To locate Lambfoot Dubb from the Corridor Route, cross Skew Gill and continue up the repaired path until you come to a series of three small gills and a broad, steep, grassy slope on the left hand. Climb until you see a small col above and slightly to your right. Here a little cairn restores confidence; just beyond is the tarn. Alternatively, follow the next promiment gill – a tributary of Greta Gill – upstream, then branch left to follow its tributary to the source, finally slanting left and upwards to the tarn. (*About 50 minutes from Styhead.*)

Foxes Tarn and Broadcrag Tarn

These two tiny ponds share the honour of being the highest named tarns in Lakeland. Although Heaton Cooper suggests that Broadcrag is the higher by nearly 50m (164ft), more recent surveys have been unable to confirm this. According to the Ordnance Survey it is not possible to give an accurate height for either. The area in which they occur was re-surveyed in the 1970s largely by means of aerial photography on a scale of 1:10,000, the contours and spot heights being interpolated by sophisticated plotting machines. Unfortunately the individual heights of the two tarns have not been recorded. A ground survey to determine their altitude would be possible but costly, so the question remains unresolved for the time being.

BROADCRAG TARN

Grid reference: 213069 Altitude: 820–830m (2,690–2,725ft) Depth: 0.5m (1½ft)

This tarn may be approached from the summit of Scafell Pike by going south-westwards down the bouldery slope towards the Cam Spout valley. A little way down, there is a small cairn and a faint track to ease the descent. A little further on, the tarn comes into view slightly to your right.

Lying on a shelf perched above the valley, sprawled between low outcrops, the marshy shores of Broadcrag Tarn bear coarse mountain and cotton grasses. Beyond, Mickledore straddles the deep trough which separates Scafell from Scafell Pike.

An approach across the scree south-eastwards from Mickledore Ridge, from where the water can just be seen, is also possible.

Broadcrag Tarn   Mist drifts across the face of Broad Stand.

(From Seathwaite allow up to 3 hours; or 25 minutes from Scafell Pike summit.)

FOXES TARN

Grid reference: 209065 Altitude: 820–830m (2,690–2,725ft) Depth: 0.5m (1½ft)

From Broadcrag Tarn, continue along the rock shelf towards Mickledore until you see a gully by which you can descend safely to the Cam Spout trough. Cross and move downhill to locate the entrance to a narrow, rock-walled, boulder-strewn gully from which issues the highest stream on the Scafell side of the valley. Climb with care to avoid dislodging loose rock, until the ascent levels out to form a short hanging valley. Here the tiny Foxes Tarn lies like a reversed question mark, a huge boulder held within its curve. Some benefactor has tried to preserve the tarn by building a low stone weir across its outflow; even so it is barely 0.5m (1½ft) deep.

Above Foxes Tarn is a zigzag path which was completed in

Foxes Tarn   To the left the scree and path lead towards Scafell.

October 1991 to replace the downward-moving scree scramble which had long threatened to extinguish the little pond for good. It took four National Trust workers 16 weeks to construct the 650m (710yd) stretch of path from the tarn to near the summit of Scafell. They had to walk 6km (3¾ miles) each way to complete every ten-hour shift. Usually they went by way of Broad Stand, a modest rock climb from Mickledore Ridge. However this is *not recommended* for the average walker. The ascent of Scafell from Mickledore via Foxes Tarn is now probably the least hazardous route. (*From Broadcrag Tarn, allow 45 minutes.*)

—————— *Tarns on the Glaramara Ridge* ——————

HIGH HOUSE TARN

Grid reference: 242093	Altitude: 663m (2,176ft)	Depth: 2m (6½ft)

In much of Lakeland there are hundreds of small, unnamed ponds, many sustaining aquatic life. Many are permanent but too small or remote or too near a larger tarn to have an identity of their own. The Glaramara–Allen Crags ridge holds several such tarns, only two of them having recorded names. High House Tarn is the largest, with a smaller pond close to it. On the Ordnance Survey map, Lincomb Tarns (in the plural) refers to nothing in particular. Heaton Cooper suggests that it should be applied to a particular favourite of his just south of High House Tarn and partially hidden among the crags of the higher ground; so be it.

I would have liked to include Tarn at Leaves in this section but because of the way maps have been drawn I have had to place it in the North-Western Region, Area E. The reason for wishing to mention it here is that the Rosthwaite Fell route, which passes Tarn at Leaves, makes an unusual and interesting approach to Glaramara and provides an alternative to the badly eroded track on the western flank of Combe Gill. (*Between Glaramara and Allen Crags, allow 1 hour.*)

Area E

This craggy, complex highland – much dissected by glacial and post-glacial erosion – forms the northern flank of the Great Langdale Valley. Eastwards towards Loughrigg Fell it narrows into a hummocky ridge separating Grasmere and Elterwater. The magnificent Stickle Tarn is accessible from Great Langdale, while on the Grasmere side are Easedale and Codale Tarns. There are many small ponds on the intervening highland as far west as Sergeant Man but only one, Lang How, is named.

STICKLE TARN, LANGDALE

Grid reference: 287076	Altitude: 469m (1,539ft)	Depth: 16m (52½ft)

Here is one of the finest corrie tarns in Lakeland, set against the great cliffs of Pavey Ark and overshadowed from the west by the dramatic heights of Harrison Stickle. With its open south-eastern aspect, it is far more welcoming than Blea Water where the classic encircling horns appear to discourage visitors.

Stickle Tarn   The view from the north-east end of Pavey Ark on the descent towards Bright Beck.

The stone-faced dam raises the water level some 2m (6½ft) but detracts little from the tarn's beauty; to its right a weir gives birth to Stickle Ghyll which falls by a series of cascades to the Langdale Valley. Beside the ghyll well-worn paths ascend from the New Dungeon Ghyll Hotel.

On a hot August day I watched from one of the two convenient car parks by the New Dungeon Ghyll Hotel as a procession of light-coloured specks moved slowly upwards; some perhaps to laze by the languid water, some to bathe, some to climb the cliffs beyond. The water is a reservoir for the hotels and cottages below; its main inflow is Bright Beck which curls in from the eastern side of Pavey Ark through a deep ravine where rowans weep.

A little way above and to the east is a small 2m (6½ft) deep unnamed peat moss tarn of still dark water, grassed to the edge. (*Allow 30–50 minutes to walk to Stickle Tarn from the car park.*)
See Walk 5

LANG HOW (HOWE) TARN
(Youdell T., Brigstone T., Robin Gill T., Silver How T.)

Grid reference: 317068	Altitude: 369m (1,210ft)	Depth: 1m (3ft)

It seems odd that such a small, overgrown tarn should acquire such a variety of names, yet remain unnamed on the Ordnance Survey map. It lies in a broad saddle on the ridge where paths cross between the valleys of Great Langdale and Easedale, and it must have been a well-known landmark in earlier times. Indeed, it was the scene of a tragedy in 1808 when George and Sarah Green lost their lives nearby during a snowstorm, leaving their six children alone for three days in Blindtarn Cottage, Easedale. Mary and Dorothy Wordsworth, who had recently moved from Dove Cottage to Allen Bank, took a hand in helping the orphans; the eldest child, Agnes, later spent some time in their service.

The tarn itself is unremarkable; in summer a broad band of rush squeezes in towards a declining circle of clear water in which an island of bright green bogbean survives. The water flows by way of Robin Gill to Langdale and the view towards the head of Langdale is impressive. Nearby, to the south-east, are three smaller, unnamed tarns.

Lang How may be reached by paths which run north-westwards along the ridge from the vicinity of High Close Youth Hostel, which stands on the summit of Red Bank on the road between Grasmere and Elterwater where there is some parking. (*About 40–60 minutes from High Close.*)

EASEDALE TARN

Grid reference: 308087	Altitude: 289m (948ft)	Depth: 21m (69ft)

I always feel that the larger tarns lack the interest and intimacy of their smaller counterparts and the contrast between Easedale and Codale Tarns is a case in point.

From the centre of Grasmere the Easedale Road passes the start of a signposted path that leads across the fields of the valley before climbing steeply beside Sourmilk Gill to the tarn. Taking this route, you arrive at the tarn outlet where moraines form a huge natural dam. On the right-hand side the great wall of Tarn Crags and Slapestone Edge falls steeply to the northern shore; ahead frown the precipices of Eagle Crag and Blea Crag. To the south the ground rises less steeply in grassy moraine mounds, from which many small streams keep the tarn supplied with water. In the little sheltered bay towards its south-western corner small white water lilies grow but generally the tarn is too deep and windswept to sustain much vegetation. Brown trout, eels and perch can be had here.

This has always been a popular tarn, as attested by the deeply grooved track. In earlier times, long-skirted ladies rode ponies to view the scene, while in the 1930s teas and mineral refreshments were sold from a small stone-built hut, now a ruin.

The path round the south side is decidedly wet and muddy; the less frequented track which follows the northern shore, is, by comparison, a much drier and more interesting route. (*From Grasmere, allow 1–1½ hours.*)

CODALE TARN

Grid reference: 297088	Altitude: 466m (1,530ft)	Depth: 2m (6½ft)

To gain this tarn, follow the muddy path westwards beyond Easedale Tarn into the hummocky zone of moraine and perched boulders. Here, a former tarn can be spotted – infilled and overgrown – betrayed by the level, marshy appearance of the ground. Climb the steep, eroded track to the left of the falls, below the prominent rock pinnacle of Belles Knott. Continue the upward scramble until you find yourself alongside the pinnacle, which will by now have transformed itself into a dinosaur's spiny back. Here a track breaks right, crosses the gill and traverses the moraine which blocks the tarn's former outlet. The water now flows out over a rock lip on the east side.

Codale is a gem of a tarn. In warm summer weather its cooling water is irresistible but, like all tarns, it has its moods. I once stood in the shelter of a boulder eating rain-sodden sandwiches, watching wind-eddies create whirlpools on the water surface then suck spray into the air and hurl it right across the tarn. Sedge, water lobelia and bur-reed are the most prominent aquatic plants, the latter patterning the water surface with its floating leaves.

The crags to the east of the tarn can be dangerous, especially in wet or misty weather. As an alternative to retracing the ascent described above, a good fine-weather return route is to go just east of north from the tarn for some 300m (330yds) towards the lowest point in the ridge ahead, following the tarn's inflow (shown on the map but not always easy to see on the ground). The route climbs gently, skirting marshy hollows, and a faint trod can be picked out on the drier sections. Just before topping the ridge, where the inlet stream is shown making a sharp elbow from the left, the track turns abruptly right or east. Continue on this line to locate the small unnamed tarns at 302093. Just below and beyond the largest one, a clear track (shown on the map as a black pecked line), descends eastwards through a rock gateway and provides a glorious, steep but safe descent over Tarn Crag and down to Easedale. (*From Easedale Tarn, allow 45–60 minutes.*)

Area F

Between the headwaters of Great Langdale and Little Langdale is some of the finest high-level walking and most magnificent scenery in Lakeland. From Bowfell and Crinkle Crags the knot of steep, rocky fells narrows eastwards to culminate in Lingmoor Fell. A great many permanent but unnamed ponds are to be found in the area of Bowfell and Crinkle Crags, one practically on the summit of the latter fell.

BLEA TARN, LANGDALE

Grid reference: 293044	Altitude: 183m (600ft)	Depth: 7m (23ft)

Blea Tarn is one of the easiest natural tarns to visit: there is a convenient car park; it is well-publicised in tourist literature; and its craggy surroundings – with the backdrop of the Langdale Pikes – give one a sense of being in the very heart of wild Lakeland. Certainly it is a scene of great beauty, especially when the rhododendrons on the rocky western shore add their charm.

'This is supposed to be the best view in the Lakes,' I once overheard a visitor say. But the relative merits of views are very

Blea Tarn (Langdale)   The view north towards Harrison Stickle.

much a matter of personal taste. Certainly this is a popular spot, especially on any sunny day in August when the footpaths around the lake are full of strolling walkers and picnic parties gather on the grassy shores. Brown trout, perch and pike inhabit the tarn.

LINGMOOR TARN

Grid reference: 302051	Altitude: 386m (1,267ft)	Depth: 1m (3ft)

Below the summit ridge of Lingmoor Fell, on the north-eastern side, Lingmoor Tarn snuggles among the moraine deposits on a shelf overlooking the Great Langdale Valley. For much of the year, brown and russet tones dominate the tarn and its surroundings, but in late summer it is transformed into a little corner of heaven. The rounded slopes and ridges descending to its shores are completely submerged by pale purple waves of heather – a scene of incredible beauty. At this time the pond still carries a few late-blooming yellow lilies but the rampant water horsetail predominates.

On the several islands there are yellow saxifrage flowers, and on one a group of stunted alder. Small runnels and seepages keep the pond supplied; an outlet trickles away to the north, then plunges down to join Great Langdale Beck.

Several modes of ascent are recorded on the Ordnance Survey map. My own preference – partly for the convenience of the Blea Tarn car park – is by means of the broad green track which begins opposite Blea Tarn House and rises diagonally right, eventually reaching the summit cairn on Brown Howes. From here the tarn can be seen and reached by a careful descent through the heather. On the ascent one may view Blea Tarn and from this angle consider Wordsworth's description of it: 'Urn-like it was in shape . . .'. (*About 1 hour to Lingmoor Tarn from Blea Tarn House.*)

LITTLE LANGDALE TARN

Grid reference: 309033	Altitude: 102m (334ft)	Depth: 8m (26ft) est.

In Little Langdale, Greenburn Beck flows out of the remains of its reservoir; and Blea Moss Beck, which empties Blea Tarn, is joined by other streams from Wrynose to form the River Brathay. These, together with other runners from Lingmoor Fell and Low Fell, flow into Little Langdale Tarn. Although there is no public access there is no lack of opportunity to view the tarn, either from the road, or better still, from the bridleway along its southern shore.

It lies within a broad, flat valley and its shoreline is low, featureless and grassy, merging with dense reed beds which grow into the lake from the south shore. The Brathay re-emerges at the eastern end and runs beneath the Slaters Bridge. The northern half of this remarkable bridge consists of lengths of slate laid horizontally, the southern is an arch cunningly contrived with slabs of slate, and the two halves meet on a small central island. The bridge is named after the generations of quarrymen who crossed the river on their way to work in the slate quarries of Tilberthwaite.

A large car park at Low Tilberthwaite makes a convenient starting point for several possible routes to the tarn. The Inn at Little Langdale provides refreshment for the return journey via Slaters Bridge. (*From Tilberthwaite, allow 1–1½ hours.*)

GREENBURN RESERVOIR (Greenburn Beck Tarn)

Grid reference: 285021	Altitude: 295m (968ft)	Depth: 2m (6½ft)

The ridge of high ground that extends from Coniston Old Man in the south, to Wetherlam at the northern end, here dips to the Greenburn Valley. A great cirque of crags encloses the head of this trough from which flows Greenburn Beck.

In the early nineteenth century, copper-mining began in the southern flank of the valley, the Tilberthwaite Fells; the drifts, spoil heaps and beckside ruins still scar the landscape. A small tarn, a swelling of the beck, was enlarged to provide a water supply for the mines, by the building of an ambitious 250m (273yd) long barrage. This is now breached near the weir so most of the water has drained away, leaving an untidy mix of marsh, shallows and deep pools, with abundant spiky rush.

A track follows Greenburn Beck up to the tarn. Start from either Slaters Bridge or Fell Foot Bridge at the bottom of Wrynose. The beck flows on east to merge with Little Langdale Tarn. (*About 1 hour.*)

RED TARN, LANGDALE

Grid reference: 268037	Altitude: 524m (1,720ft)	Depth: 1.5m (5ft)

From the summit of Wrynose, near the Three Shires Stone, a prominent path leads northwards towards Crinkle Crags, passing along the way this delightful, elongated tarn. It lies among glacial drift on a broad saddle below Pike o'Blisco and is shallow for its size; the bottom is stony and the water clear, but I saw no sign of its reputed trout. Strap-like leaves of floating bur-reed sprawl over much of its surface in summer. A short slow beck flows in from the south and groundwater no doubt filters in from the steep slopes on either side. Perhaps the tarn derives its name from the colour of the rocks nearby.

In the area between Cold Pike, Great Knott and Crinkle Crags there are many small, unnamed tarns lurking among the bouldery terrain: one small tarn exists almost on the summit of Crinkle Crags itself. A further scattering of tiny gems may be found east of Pike o'Blisco, in the Wrynose Fell and Blake Rigg area. (*Allow 45 minutes from Wrynose summit to Red Tarn.*)

THREE TARNS, BOWFELL (Tarns of Buscoe)

Grid reference: 248060	Altitude: 720m (2,363ft)	Depth: 1m (3ft)

On the broad, flat col between Crinkle Crags and Bowfell lie three small ponds in shallow depressions in the glacial debris. (Alas, only two when I passed by.) These tarns might warrant no more attention than the many unnamed ponds scattered to the south-

Three Tarns (Bowfell) A view of one of the tarns looking west towards the Scafells.

west of Crinkle Crags, except for the fact that they stand at the intersection of several busy paths and are also situated at one of the finest viewpoints in the Lake District.

Here is the meeting point for routes crossing from Upper Eskdale to Great Langdale and the ridgeway northwards from Crinkle Crags, over Bowfell and on towards Esk Hause. From these tarns you can see some of Lakeland's finest rock scenery; to the east stand the Pikes of Langdale, while westwards rise the mighty Scafells and linking Mickledore. (*From Red Tarn, allow 1–1½ hours.*)

Area G

The following tarns are to be found near Coniston Old Man at the south-eastern extremity of the Borrowdale Volcanic Group rocks, and they are most easily accessible from Coniston. Seathwaite Tarn is rather out on a limb and best reached from the Duddon Valley but cannot easily be linked with the other Dunnerdale tarns included in Area I. The walking here is less rugged than in Areas D, E and F but the weather conditions can be equally unpredictable.

BOO TARN

Grid reference: 283968	Altitude: 280m (920ft)	Depth: 0.5m (1½ft)

Every year thousands of walkers pass this tiny tarn without being aware of its presence. Although Boo Tarn is located beside the much-frequented Walna Scar Road above Coniston, it is so overgrown with rush that only a careful search will reveal it during the summer. If it did not have such a long-established and recorded name it would surely be forgotten.

This marshy pond is held by a track-side moraine and its water seeps down from the slopes of Coniston Old Man; a small outlet stream runs south-westwards into Hussey Well Beck.

To reach this and the following tarns, leave Coniston by the uphill road opposite Lake Road. Bear left up a steeper, narrow lane and go along for 1km (½ mile) to the fell gate. Beyond is the Walna Scar Road. The tarn is just over 500m (550yds) beyond. (*About 45 minutes from Coniston.*) See **Walk 6**.

BLIND TARN, CONISTON

Grid reference: 263967	Altitude: 559m (1,834ft)	Depth: 7m (23ft)

Tucked precariously beneath Brown Pike in a kind of pouch, with a narrow moraine to hold it in place lest it spill over into the cove below, this little gem of a tarn is circular and full of fish. They rose energetically during my midday visit; one trout seen near the shore looked to be at least 20cm (8in.) in length. As well as trout, small char are found here, both emigrés from Coniston perhaps. As the tarn is 'blind', with no surface water flowing in or out, their residence here is certainly involuntary; considering the sparseness of vegetation in the pond, their survival is remarkable.

The easiest route is to follow the Walna Scar Road past Boo Tarn and cross the track and beck which descend from Goat's Water. Where the road begins to steepen and Walna Scar comes into view ahead, keep an eye open for a grassy track on the right which leads through an abandoned quarry to Blind Tarn. (*About 45 minutes from Boo Tarn.*) See **Walk 6**.

GOAT'S WATER

Grid reference: 266976	Altitude: 503m (1,650ft)	Depth: 13m (47ft)

My visit to Goat's Water coincided with a single persistent cloud that kept the sun covered. An icy breeze from the region of Goat's Hawse rippled the tarn's surface, causing a continual, busy lapping. The water appeared cold and inhospitable, with none of the charm of little Blind Tarn nearby.

The outflow emerges from beneath a mosaic of massive boulders avalanched from the black cliffs of Dow Crag in earlier times. These boulders form a natural dam and perhaps deepen the water of an ice-scoured basin. The serrated skyline of the cliffs above the western shore contrast with the smoother slopes – steep but grassy and with occasional grey outcrops – that rise to Coniston Old Man.

The water contains small but plentiful trout and a few char, though the plant life is sparse – floating bur-reed and water starwort being the principal aquatics.

Having trekked this far, it's well worth continuing to the Old Man by way of Goat's Hawse in order to collect the bonus of Low Water Tarn on the descent. (*From Boo Tarn, allow 50 minutes.*) **See Walk 6.**

LOW WATER

Grid reference: 275983	Altitude: 544m (1,785ft)	Depth: 14m (46ft)

How cool and inviting Low Water's blue-green depths appear during a hot summer's descent from the summit of Coniston Old Man. Facing north-east, set deep in moraine, and overhung by Buckbarrow Crags, this fine cirque tarn has an impressive air of mystery. Sadly, this is soon shattered by the noisy stream of pilgrims ascending and descending the white eroded track nearby. The tiered spoil heaps and the stone-faced dam with its protruding iron pipe tell of slate-quarrying activities in the recent past.

The tarn is fed by three gills draining from the crags and the outflow, Low Water Beck, forms an impressive cascade of nearly 150m (500ft) which joins Levers Water Beck and eventually Church Beck to flow through the centre of Coniston town. I am told there are trout but aquatic vegetation is sparse, consisting mainly of water starwort. (*Allow 1–1½ hours from Goat's Water via the Old Man.*) **See Walk 6.**

LEVERS WATER

Grid reference: 279993	Altitude: 414m (1,358ft)	Depth: 38m (125ft)

In size, shape, setting and aspect, Levers Water has much in common with Stickle Tarn. The surrounding crags are less continuous and dramatic than those at Great Langdale's premier tarn, but they seem to press in more closely. The stone-faced dam and spillway almost replicate those at Stickle.

Although originally a natural tarn, Levers Water has for centuries provided water for power and processing in Copper-mines Valley. (A water treatment plant built below the dam in the 1970s now provides the domestic water supply for Coniston town and other settlements on either side of the lake.) As a reservoir, the tarn is subject to seasonal fluctuations in its water level and this probably accounts for the absence of aquatic plants around its margins. It is more than twice as deep as Stickle and the water is said to be well-stocked with small brown trout.

The tarn is situated some 3km (2 miles) north-east of Coniston and can be reached by following Church Beck upstream from the bridge in the centre of the town. There are two possible routes, one from each side of the bridge. That on the true left of the beck (in this case, keeping the beck on your left hand) begins from the Black Bull Hotel as a metalled lane, then deteriorates into an unsurfaced road skirting the grounds of Holywath. The road on the other side of the bridge leads to the Sun Inn. From here, bear right, pass through the farm gate and follow the rough, steep track to Miner's Bridge where the former track may be joined. Just beyond, the valley levels out to a broad, desolate area of abandoned spoil heaps, a terrace of miner's cottages and the youth hostel which is housed in the former Coppermines Office. Beyond the hostel, the track rises steeply, winding up past the water treatment plant, until you gain the lip of the corrie which holds the tarn. (*Allow 1–1½ hours from Coniston.*) See **Walk 6**.

SEATHWAITE TARN

Grid reference: 254987	Altitude: 370m (1,214ft)	Depth: 24m (79ft)

At one time a smaller, natural tarn, this water was enlarged to function as a reservoir supplying water to the Barrow area. The concrete dam wall, buttressed with stacked slate, extends for some 350m (380yds) in a graceful curve, to merge with the natural contours at either end. The date '1907' is inscribed on the lintel of a small building which stands at the foot of the dam. The Duddon is used as a conduit, the water being abstracted at a weir further downstream to be piped to Barrow.

There is a single rocky islet towards the northern end of the tarn. On its eastern side the bouldery fell rises steeply upwards towards Dow Crag, invisible beyond the slope. Brown trout abound; the fishing is controlled by the Furness Fishing Association.

Several possible approaches are shown on the Ordnance Survey map; my own favourite is from the very convenient Dunnerdale

Forest car park. From here, walk northwards along the road to Pike Howe Close and enter the plantation by the forest road, doubling back along a path a short distance into the plantation. Follow the path down, cross the beck, and once clear of the woodland, climb the eastern slope, contouring below White Howe and Little Blake Rigg, to swing eastwards into the Tarn Beck valley. The going is a little wet at times but improves as you get nearer the tarn. (*Allow 1½ hours from the car park.*)

Area H

Except for Caw Moss, the following tarns are situated on the gentler Silurian rocks beside Coniston Water, Arnsbarrow on the eastern side, the rest above the western shore.

TORVER TARN
(Torver Reservoir, Thrang Moss Reservoir)

Grid reference: 281926	Altitude: 116m (380ft)	Depth: 8m (26ft) est.

This is one of my favourite waters. Labelled 'Reservoir Disused' on the Ordnance Survey map, it has a small dam and once supplied water power for a nearby bobbin mill. Even so, it is a natural tarn and contains a sufficient variety of aquatic plants to provide something of interest throughout the summer. Yellow flag irises grace the water's edge while small white water lilies dot the surface, sharing the southern end with broadleaved pondweed and thrusting water horsetail. Along the eastern shore, water lobelia flowers and spike rushes wave their short, ebony-tipped spears. Beneath the surface ghostly grey armies of water milfoil sway gently. The northern end has deeper, open water devoid of plants. The only blight on all this beauty is an electrical power line which follows the eastern shore.

The tarn is well hidden between low, parallel ridges until the explorer lights upon its lip; the A5084 road by Coniston Water is very close, yet Torver Tarn's presence is unsuspected by the flocks of tourists who pass on their way to the lake shore. To reach it from the A5084, cross Torver Beck by the bridge (marked 'stepping stones' on the Ordnance Survey map), then follow Mere Beck – and another electrical power line – until a small stream flows in steeply from the right. Follow this to the dam. (*About 30–50 minutes from the road.*)

BIRK HAW and
TARNS ON TORVER LOW COMMON

Grid reference: 269924	Altitude: 180m (590ft)	Depth: 3m (10ft)

Several small ponds, of which only Birk Haw is named, exist to the west of Torver Tarn and are recorded on the Ordnance Survey map. They hide between the steep, low north–south ridges which are a feature of the common, and some amusement can be had locating and exploring them. They are well vegetated and you may enjoy identifying the common emergents there.

CAW MOSS TARN

Grid reference: 253948	Altitude: 385m (1,263ft)	Depth: 1.5m (5ft)

After several days of heavy November rain I was rash enough to visit this peat bog tarn, surrounded at the time by a large boot-filling quagmire. It is located between Torver and the Duddon Valley and beyond the southern extremity of Walna Scar. About 1.5km (1 mile) south-west of Torver, Hummer Lane branches right from the A593; 2km (1¼ miles) along on the right-hand side is

a Forestry Commission plantation with two roadside car parks. The first of these is a convenient place to pick up the blue arrowed path beginning at the south-eastern entrance to the woodland (shown as a green pecked line on the Ordnance Survey map). The path wanders westward to gain the western boundary road which should be followed to Natty Bridge at the northern boundary. Beyond the bridge the path continues but after 100m (110yds) you should take the sharp right-hand branch which crosses open moor, winding between rock outcrops but staying roughly parallel with the forest boundary. Eventually it passes through a gap in a stone wall where the tarn has its main inflow.

The pond lies at the base of a long outcrop and has two

extensions at right angles. Due to the flooded conditions on the day of my visit its outline was somewhat blurred and several temporary satellite tarns were spread about the surrounding moorland. The water was clear, the peaty rim slanting to a gravel bottom populated by shoreweed and sedge. Human intervention was evident in the two manholes at the south-eastern end and a channel extending downhill towards the Broughton Moor Quarries. (*Allow 1½ hours from the road.*)

KELLY HALL TARN

Grid reference: 288933	Altitude: 119m (390ft)	Depth: 1.5m (5ft)

This small, well-vegetated tarn lies hidden among bracken-covered mounds of glacial debris, within 200m (220yds) of the Torver to Blawith A5084 road. A footpath just opposite the roadside garage will lead you to this somewhat featureless water. At the south end a small dam has been added to increase its volume and a prominent sign tells us that the water is used for drinking and

Kelly Hall Tarn   A small pond with a fine view towards the Coniston Fells.

requests no swimming. The name is derived from a nearby building, now demolished. (*About 10 minutes from the road.*)

LONG MOSS TARN

Grid reference: 292936	Altitude: 131m (430ft)	Depth: 1m (3ft)

The name is very apt, for this tarn is indeed long and mossy. Its southern section is overgrown with rush and cotton grass, while the northern half contains more open water and a rich growth of white water lilies. Confined in a narrow valley between low ridges, the tarn can be reached by continuing along the footpath from Kelly Hall Tarn. Both ponds appear to be seldom visited. (*About 10 minutes from Kelly Hall Tarn.*)

ARNSBARROW TARN

Grid reference: 311917	Altitude: 295m (968ft)	Depth: 1.5m (5ft)

Seen first from Top o' Selside, this was a small, almost circular, amethyst-blue water, set in the middle of a shallow amphitheatre. The shores were fringed with the segmented stems of water horsetail. Small lily pads shouldered a space between them and displayed a few impoverished white blooms here and there. Standing quietly beside the tarn I was aware of considerable activity over and above the hum of bees on the still abundant heather. Three whirligig beetles, bright as jewels, whirled about one another in a patterned dance on the water surface. But the principal actors were the dragonflies, hovering in their green and black livery, ready to dart away on the instant after any rival foolhardy enough to intrude into their favoured inlet. These encounters, fast and ferocious, were accompanied by the rattle of wings colliding like wooden swords in a mock battle. The smaller electric-blue damsel flies shared the stage, apparently unhindered.

Disappointingly, the film in my camera failed to wind on, so a clearance after morning rain tempted me to revisit Arnsbarrow the following day. On this occasion brilliant sunshine and shadows driven by a stiff breeze conspired to create a very different scene. The ruffled surface of the water reflected a deep, deep blue, while the wind-curled edges of the lily pads flashed bright against the darker wavelets. A solitary swift passed nearby, but – except for the swish of wind through the sedge and water horsetail – all seemed still. Yesterday's dragonflies were gone.

Despite the boldly marked footpath on the Ordnance Survey map, the tarn would seem to be seldom visited as the trods are narrow. Eastwards, beyond the tarn, the forest fence of Grizedale can be glimpsed. Arnsbarrow Tarn is not easy to locate and finding parking is always difficult. It's best to start from the National Trust Nibthwaite car park at 296098. A forest track leads away from the rear of the car park, taking you roughly east, then north. After winding to and fro, it eventually ends at a stile, beyond which is a stony track beside Selside Beck. Follow this bridle path northwards until Peel Island comes into view on the lake below, then look out for a pile of stones on the right which marks the point where you should leave the path and take the sheep trod up, angling leftwards. Make for the summit cairn on Top o' Selside from where the tarn can be seen. (*Allow 1–1½ hours from Nibthwaite car park.*)

Area I

The remote Dunnerdale Fells of South Cumbria, east of Ulpha and the River Duddon, are accessible only by steep and narrow fell roads. The fell road north from Broughton Mills to Dunnerdale climbs steadily to a halfway summit at Kiln Bank Cross, before descending to the Duddon Valley. At Kiln Bank Cross is a level area offering generous parking and from this high point the rugged nature of the surrounding Borrowdale Volcanic country can be seen to advantage. Ridges of uplifted strata are crested by jagged teeth of grey rock; between the ridges, steep vales and bracken slopes descend to boggy bottoms. Abandoned mine tips to the east offer good pickings for the mineral collector but westward lie the tarns. Stickle Tarn is to be found beneath the intriguing pyramid of Stickle Pike, while Tarn Hill boasts a collection of eight ponds (well, seven ponds and one bog really) of differing appeal.

STICKLE TARN, DUDDON

Grid reference: 214928	Altitude: 305m (1,000ft)	Depth: 3m (10ft)

There is a broad green path on either side of the Broughton Mills to Dunnerdale fell road, at Kiln Bank Cross. Follow the westward extension for 100m (110yds), then branch left and uphill, following another prominent green track. Ahead, an eroded path continues to the three-topped summit of Stickle Pike. It is a point of honour when visiting the tarn to ascend this hill, at 375m (1,231ft) the highest in this group of fells. The tarn is on your left, with views beyond to Morecambe Bay.

Roughly triangular in shape, with an open aspect towards its southern outflow end, this natural tarn occupies what might almost be a shallow corrie, scooped between steeply angled strata. There is no surface inflow but a musical beck emerges beside the small end moraine.

Myriad whirligig beetles busied themselves around the water's edge and green-bodied damsel flies rose in clouds as I moved beside the rushes. Bur-reed was here, and bogbean, water horsetail, broadleaved pondweed and the tiny, buttercup-like lesser spearwort. A bonny tarn. (*About 20 minutes from the road.*)

THE EIGHT TARNS OF TARN HILL

Grid reference: 209920	Altitudes: 260–300m (850–980ft)

From Stickle Tarn, return to the broad green track and continue along it in a south-south-westerly direction, skirting the head of the valley of Hare Hall Beck and crossing a low ridge; ahead, the prominent outline of Tarn Hill with its summit cairn beckons. Aim for the northern end of this remarkable hill.

Grouped around the summit cairn, the tarns are listed here as I first encountered them, beginning with the northernmost one and moving in a clockwise direction (see diagram). (*From Stickle Tarn to Tarn Hill summit, allow 45 minutes.*)

Tarn 1

A deep hollow gouged in the rock of the ridge holds this shallow, peaty tarn at the northern end of the hill. It contains bogbean, cotton grass and plenty of spiky rush.

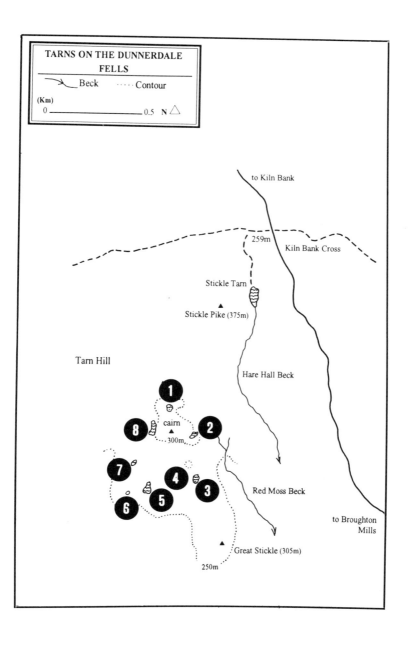

TARNS ON THE DUNNERDALE
FELLS

Beck ···· Contour

(Km)
0 _____ 0.5 N △

to Kiln Bank

259m

Kiln Bank Cross

Stickle Tarn

Stickle Pike (375m)

Tarn Hill

Hare Hall Beck

1

cairn

8   300m

2

7

4

5   **3**

6

Red Moss Beck

to Broughton
Mills

Great Stickle (305m)

250m

Tarn 2

If you move south to the summit cairn it is possible to see six of the tarns. Face south and the nearest one is slightly to your left, a remarkable pond of about 1m (3ft) in depth, brimful, yet with hardly any catchment. It reaches to the very edge of the steep slope. Look along its length to see Stickle Pike beyond. Spread upon its surface are the long, slim floating leaves of bur-reed – unique among this group of tarns.

Tarn 3

A shallow tarn this, with a small grassy island. Small degenerate leaves of bogbean grow in this very dull depression.

Tarn 4

Although shown prominently on the Ordnance Survey map, this tarn is almost completely overgrown. From the summit cairn looking south, it appears to be simply an area of bog.

Tarn 5

Elongated and deep, this tarn is devoid of vegetation except at its southern end where there is a vigorous growth of bogbean.

Tarn 6

Again, bogbean predominates in this small shallow pool of mini-islands; some pondweed grows here also.

Tarn 7

Another shallow pool similar to Tarn 6 in its vegetation.

Tarn 8

This is the largest of the tarns, the whole surface dotted with the three-fingered hands of bogbean thrust aloft as if in supplication. Tiny peaty islands abound, sprinkled with bright yellow saxifrage. The pond extends to the very edge of a sheer rock precipice. From Tarn 7 below, no one would suspect its suspended presence.

The Tarns
of North-East
Lakeland

The following 16 tarns may be found with the aid of the Outdoor Leisure 5 Ordnance Survey map. They are located in the Ullswater–Haweswater areas and lie mainly on Borrowdale Volcanic Group rocks. Altitude falls rapidly eastwards from the high point of the Helvellyn ridge to Ullswater, rises again to the High Street ridge, then declines steadily to the Lowther Valley. There are now only 16 tarns here, which I have divided into three convenient groups. Areas A and B may be reached from the Ullswater Valley, as may Red Crag Tarn, although – for the sake of convenience – it has been incorporated into Area C, the Haweswater group.

Though the tarns are few in number, they are certainly high in quality, for this group contains Blea Water and Red Tarn, two of the finest corrie tarns in Lakeland. Of the others, Angle Tarn is surely the most interesting and attractive of all ridge tarns; Hard Tarn offers a challenge for the walker; Kepple Cove has a dramatic story to tell; while Grisedale Tarn has poignant associations with the Wordsworth family.

Although they no longer exist, Sticks and Kepple Cove Tarns are mentioned in the text in order to complete the record.

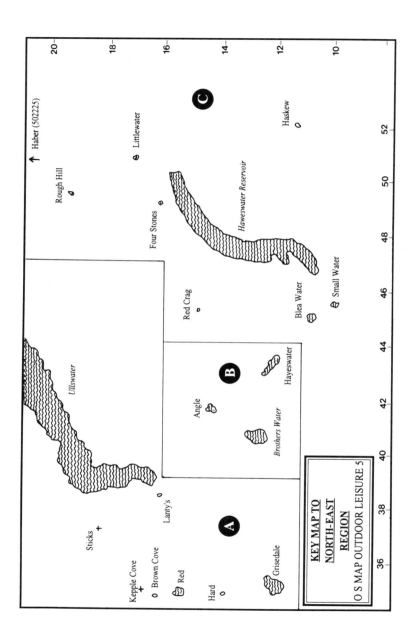

KEY MAP TO
NORTH-EAST
REGION

O S MAP OUTDOOR LEISURE 5

Haber (502225)

Rough Hill

Littlewater

Four Stones

C

Haskew

Ullswater

Sticks

Kepple Cove

Brown Cove

Red

Hard

Lanty's

Grisedale

Red Crag

Haweswater Reservoir

Blea Water

Small Water

Angle

Hayeswater

B

Brothers Water

A

10 12 14 16 18 20

36 38 40 42 44 46 48 50 52

Area A

The seven tarns in Area A are to be found on that great ridge that extends northwards from Ambleside and declines to Matterdale Common and the A66. To the west it is bounded by Dunmail Raise, Thirlmere and the A591; to the east by the Kirkstone Pass, Ullswater and the A592. There are four fells in Lakeland which rise to or exceed the significant altitude of 914.4m (3,000ft) and one of these, Helvellyn, is to be found here. The term 'cove' is preferred here to combe or comb to refer to a corrie.

RED TARN, HELVELLYN

Grid reference: 348152	Altitude: 718m (2,356ft)	Depth: 25m (82ft)

Below the summit of Helvellyn on its eastern side, held within the enclosing arms of Striding Edge and Swirral Edge, is Red Tarn, perhaps one of the best-known tarns of Lakeland. Brown trout and schelly (a rare type of freshwater herring) exist here and William Wordsworth is said to have fished these waters.

Because of its popularity this place has frequently been the scene of tragedy. Striding Edge has been the main culprit, particularly when snow powders the crags. The oft-related tale of Charles Gough and his faithful dog is one of the earliest recorded fatalities here; an account of the accident was much publicised at the time, in 1805, and immortalised in poetry by both Wordsworth and Sir Walter Scott. For details of the dog's three-month vigil beside his dead master, first walk Striding Edge, then refer to the memorial slab as you gain the summit.

The tarn is fed by several small runners from the back wall of the corrie and the outflow emerges from the front, or east side. In the mid 1800s the tarn was dammed with boulders to raise the level and supply water via leats or channels (traces of which can still be seen) to the upper Glenridding Beck and from thence to the Greenside lead mines.

The most convenient approach is by way of the Striding Edge track from Glenridding. Leave this path at the Hole-in-the-Wall and follow the easy peat track to the tarn. Alternatively, visit

Lanty's Tarn first, then follow the path westward beside the wall to join the Striding Edge path. (*Allow 1½–2 hours from Glenridding to Red Tarn.*)

GRISEDALE TARN

Grid reference: 348120	Altitude: 539m (1,769ft)	Depth: 34m (111½ft)

Grisedale Tarn is almost identical to Red Tarn in size and shape but very different in setting. Whereas Red Tarn is held in a corrie, this water lies in a great depression at the apex of three valleys, overlooked by the intervening highland. It contains brown trout, perch and eels, but plant life is sparse.

The outflow emerges at the north-eastern end and flows down the long Grisedale Valley to Patterdale and Ullswater. To the west, between Seat Sandal and Dollywagon Pike, is the valley of Raise Beck which falls to Dunmail Raise and provides the shortest approach to the tarn. (*About 30–45 minutes from the summit of the pass on the A591.*) Up this steep path was borne the crown of the defeated King Dunmail, killed or captured by the Romans. His crown is said to have been cast into the steely waters of the tarn.

To the south, you can cross Grisedale Hause to take the path to Grasmere via Tongue Gill. On 20 September 1800, William and Dorothy Wordsworth walked up this path to the tarn with their sailor brother John, who was returning to London to rejoin his ship. Just beyond the outflow they parted, John never again to return to Grasmere. His ship, an East Indiaman bound for the Far East, sank in the English Channel two years later, with the loss of 300 lives. This poignant tale is recorded on the Brothers' Parting Stone just below the outflow from the tarn, though the inscription is now difficult to read. Interestingly, John Wordsworth's ship was the subject of one of the earliest salvage operations using a diving bell; his sword can be seen at Rydal Mount.

Near Mill Bridge, at the bottom of Dunmail Raise, take the signed path – an old packhorse road via Tongue Gill – to the tarn. (*Allow 1–1½ hours.*)

Perhaps the finest approach is the beautiful walk from Patterdale, following Grisedale Beck and overlooked by the magnificent mountain scenery of the Helvellyn range and St Sunday Crag. (*Allow 1½–2 hours.*)

LANTY'S TARN

Grid reference: 384163	Altitude: 276m (905ft)	Depth: 2m (6½ft)

The ridge which separates the Glenridding and Grisedale valleys narrows at its eastern extremity where it terminates abruptly in cliffs that abut the lake – shorn or truncated by the Ullswater Glacier. At this end of the ridge, on a gentle col, is Lanty's Tarn, once a smaller natural pond owned by Lancelot Dobson (hence 'Lanty's') who lived at Grassthwaite Howe. It was acquired by the Marshalls of Patterdale Hall who enlarged it by damming the outflow, then used it for fishing in summer and collecting ice in winter. The ice was stored for summer use in the ice house which still stands near the end of the tarn.

The water itself is overhung by birch trees; while Scots pines

Lanty's Tarn   The dam and ice house are located at the far end.

stand sternly in the background. Even on a dull day I found this little tarn attractive. Sedge and spike rush edge the water and broadleaved pondweed spreads across the surface; but whether the trout, originally transferred from the lake, still dart and hide there I could not say.

From the track which runs along the south side of Glenridding Beck from the road bridge, a steep path climbs to the tarn. (*Allow 30–45 minutes from Glenridding car park.*)

HARD TARN

Grid reference: 346138	Altitude: 693m (2,274ft)	Depth: 1m (3ft)

This gem of a tarn is notoriously hard to find – and to clamber up to – but well worth the effort. It appears to contain the clearest water of any tarn in Lakeland; but, should you dare to swim, you will soon stir up its dark deposits. At the back of the pond a thin forest of pale green water starwort touches the surface, adding colour and interest. Behind rises a 10m (33ft) crag; another falls away below the rock lip so that the tarn appears to be poised upon a rock shelf with a slight backward tilt. A shallow water-worn groove allows a gentle outflow to trickle over the lip and away downhill. Maintained by seepage, the tarn lies in Ruthwaite Cove, between Nethermost and Cock Coves, below High Crag.

The best approach is from the remains of Ruthwaite Lodge beside the track which follows Grisedale Beck about 1km (½ mile) below Grisedale Tarn. Behind the lodge a faint track leads uphill through bracken into the lower cove. From here, follow the main beck until it bears away to the left; then continue straight on, following the lesser stream until you emerge on to a fairly level ledge at the base of the final screes descending from the High Crag–Nethermost Pike ridge. Move to the right to a boggy patch and pools; then continue to a long ice-smoothed bolster of rocks, below which is Hard Tarn. (*From Grisedale Tarn or Patterdale, allow 1–1½ hours.*)

Experienced walkers may enjoy finishing their visit by ascending to Nethermost Pike via the interesting little ridge which forms an arête between Ruthwaite and Nethermost Coves. From the tarn, move to the right, or east-north-east, until the ridge becomes obvious, then climb with care.

STICKS TARN (Top Dam)

Grid reference: 357181	Altitude: 548m (1,799ft)	Depth: 1.5m (5ft)

Sadly, like Kepple Cove Tarn, this tarn no longer exists – apart, that is, from a momentary slowing and swelling of Sticks Beck. Now one may only stand upon the remnants of the considerable stone-faced barrage which held the former tarn and gaze at the waving pondweed, then at the breach through which the beck escapes. Shortly after passing through the gap the water disappears below ground, to surface lower down the steepening valley as Swart Beck which then joins Glenridding Beck.

According to the 1958 edition of the one-inch Ordnance Survey Lake District National Park map on which it is shown, the tarn almost equalled Small Water in surface area. It is not surprising therefore that Heaton Cooper mentions that it held trout, which once gave pleasure to the local miners. A small natural water apparently existed here, but the changed contours of the land surface make it impossible to distinguish its former outline.

Sticks Pass, the highest in Lakeland, zigzags up from Greenside to the floor of the hanging valley where the remnants of former mining activity and the breached barrage may be seen. Ahead, the pass – so named because of the stakes used to mark its route – winds to the summit of the ridge between Raise and Stybarrow Dodd before descending to Thirlmere.

(From Glenridding car park, allow 1 hour. From the vicinity of Greenside Youth Hostel the pass is clearly signposted.)

KEPPLE COVE TARN

Grid reference: 345165	Altitude: 550m (1,805ft)	Depth: Nil

This tarn disappeared very suddenly; it was there on Friday 28 October 1927 – the following day it was gone.

The lead mines at Greenside used large quantities of water for processing the ore. This was obtained from Glenridding Beck, its level being maintained by water stored in Red Tarn and Kepple Cove Tarn. An iron pipe was driven through the steep, narrow earth dam which held Kepple Cove Tarn, water being drawn off each day as required. However a severe overnight storm led to the dam being breached in the early hours of Saturday. The resultant surge of water swept down Glenridding Beck, wreaking havoc in the sleeping village of Glenridding. The details are recorded in the Visitors' Centre there. Although the village has long since recovered, the breached dam still abruptly interrupts the path to Brown Cove, as if the flood had occurred only yesterday.

Kepple Cove is to the side and faces into the main valley, its upper rim encircled by steep grey walls, from which scree descends to a green velvety bottom where the almost circular tarn once lay. Across the former tarn bed a slow stream flows between spiky rush, its shallows sustaining a dense growth of pondweed, starwort and other aquatic plants not usually present in a mountain beck – survivors, perhaps, of that departed water. (*From Glenridding car park, allow 35–45 minutes.*)

BROWN COVE TARN

Grid reference: 343160	Altitude: 615m (2,019ft)	Depth: 1m (3ft)

Barely 500m (550yds) beyond Kepple Cove at the head of the valley is Brown Cove, almost completely hemmed in by the steep flanks of Helvellyn, Swirral Edge and Catstycam which together form a wild, rocky skyline. Only open to the north, this must be the most sun-bereft combe in Lakeland.

A broad stone-faced dam built around 1860 fronts what remains of the reservoir which once stored water for the Greenside mines. There are two linked shallow ponds of irregular shape, probably bearing little resemblance to any natural tarn that might once have existed here. The impounded water of the former reservoir has rendered the bottom of the cove as flat as the proverbial pancake; now covered in short fine grass, this would make a respectable cricket pitch.

The ponds contain clear shallow water on a gravel and mud bed, and – with the addition of shoreweed – the vegetation is similar to that found in the beck at Kepple Cove. Surplus water now seeps below the dam to form the source of Glenridding Beck. An old 66cm (24in) iron pipe, fitted with a valve, passes through the dam wall; this was used to control the supply for the mines downstream.

Nearby, the north-west ridge of Catstycam leads steeply but safely on to Swirral Edge. From here, you can go on to Red Tarn or Helvellyn summit, or return to Glenridding by following the path beside Red Tarn Beck. (*About 15–20 minutes from Kepple Cove to Brown Cove Tarn.*)

Area B

East of the A592 Ullswater–Kirkstone Pass line, Lakeland once more bares its Borrowdale Volcanic teeth, best exposed in the ridges and arêtes above the head of Haweswater, before declining beneath the more recent Carboniferous deposits eastwards beyond the River Lowther. This central highland is penetrated by steep-sided valleys to produce a confusing tangle of ridges, dominated by the north–south whaleback followed by High Street, the Roman road which narrows to a couple of metres at the Straits (or Straights, depending upon which Ordnance Survey map is used) of Riggindale.

HAYESWATER

Grid reference: 432122	Altitude: 425m (1,395ft)	Depth: 16m (52½ft)

Elongated in shape, and pressed within the steep confines of this somewhat sombre vale, Hayeswater is more akin to a glacial valley finger lake than a corrie. The surplus water exits via a stepped spillway-cum-dam; its reservoir role is confirmed by a water treatment plant beside the gill, which you pass on your way to the tarn. The villages of Ullswater valley receive their domestic supply from here and the water even helps to fulfil Penrith's requirements. The fishing, for trout and perch, is restricted to members of the Penrith Angling Association.

Originally a natural feature, the tarn may be approached on either side of the delightful Hayeswater Gill: either by crossing the bridge above its confluence with Pasture Beck; or by continuing on the partially metalled road to the treatment plant, skirting the building to the right and descending the track to a foot-bridge over the gill. The track then rises to join the rough road to the tarn.

Hayeswater High Street (the Roman road) runs along the ridge beyond.

As well as Hayeswater, there is much delightful walking in the area, with Angle Tarn, Blea Water and Caudale Head Tarns all within easy reach.

Parking is plentiful; one car park is by Cow Bridge, just north of Brothers Water, 10 minutes from Hartsop. The other is at the far end of the village itself. (*The tarn is about 25–35 minutes from Hartsop.*) **See Walk 7**.

ANGLE TARN, PATTERDALE

Grid reference: 417144	Altitude: 480m (1,576ft)	Depth: 9m (29½ft)

How different is this tarn from its namesake by Bowfell. The latter is set in a fine corrie, whereas Angle Tarn sprawls in a great amphitheatre set high above Ullswater. With low crags to the west, grassy slopes to the east and its islands, promontories and bays, Angle Tarn offers an eye-catching variety of form and colour.

The approach from Patterdale is perhaps the most interesting.

Although parking is always difficult the early bird may find a layby. (The car park at Glenridding is expensive and adds about 1.5km each way to the trek.) Cross to the east side of the valley by the rough track near Patterdale School and ascend south-eastwards to Boredale Hause with views of the Helvellyn range on your right. At the Hause, cross Stonebarrow Gill and continue on the track in a generally southerly direction round the head of Dubhow Beck, then skirt Angle Tarn Pikes to find the tarn. One is immediately aware of the tranquillity and solitude of this place. Energetic streams from north and south maintain the tarn, while Angletarn Beck drains westward to the Ullswater Valley. (*Allow 1–1½ hours from Patterdale.*)

The alternative approach from Hartsop offers more convenient parking. Ascend first to Hayeswater; from the outflow climb diagonally northwards to gain the track from The Knott to Satura and Black Crags, and on to the tarn. (*About 1–1½ hours.*) **See Walk 7.**

Area C

The following tarns are on the eastern fringe of the Lake District and best approached from the Haweswater area. Parking is limited and the little car park at Mardale Head is always over-crowded, for here is some of Lakeland's best walking and most attractive scenery.

RED CRAG TARN

Grid reference: 451150	Altitude: 700m (2,298ft)	Depth: 1m (3ft)

On the northern section of the long Roman road – commonly called High Street – which traverses the high ground of the eastern fells, between Ravens Howe and Red Crag, is Red Crag Tarn, the larger of two ponds and the only water on the Street. Its distant glint can be seen from the summit of High Raise, 1km (½ mile) away. It occupies a hollow in the much-dissected peat surface, and a handy wooden stake enabled me to estimate its depth. It was brimful, with sheer margins, so I was able to plumb the bedrock within an easy arm's length. Around most of the circumference the depth seemed to be just under 1m (3ft). No plants grew in the dull, opaque water and there was little to commend it apart from a thriving community of water skaters.

The shortest routes to Red Crag Tarn are from Hartsop or Mardale Head which both offer convenient parking. My own choice is to go from Hartsop via Hayeswater. Begin by crossing Hayeswater Gill at the outflow and climb steeply, then circle round The Knott to the Straits of Riggindale. Here, take the track which branches left, and skirt the head of Riggindale Valley. Then bear left again to head for High Raise and the tarn.

The alternative route from Mardale Head crosses Mardale Beck to follow the shore around The Rigg, then over Riggindale Beck, ascending Kidsty Howes and Pike to join High Street. A good return route takes you along the superb ridge over Riggindale Crags, finally descending to The Rigg.

On either route one can play 'spot the Golden Eagle'. (*Allow 1½–2½ hours from either Hartsop or Mardale Head.*)

BLEA WATER

Grid reference: 449108	Altitude: 483m (1,585ft)	Depth: 63m (207ft)

Perhaps the most impressive of Lakeland's tarns, Blea Water crouches within its near-circular corrie of towering crags and enclosing horns of crescentic moraine. Exceeded in depth only by the lakes of Windermere and Wastwater, it is certainly the deepest of the tarns; its already considerable depth has been increased by the addition of a dam to provide compensation water for Haweswater Reservoir. Only water starwort occurs here but there are small brown trout and some perch.

There is parking at Mardale Head, from where you can cross Mardale Beck and approach the tarn by way of the rising path above Bleawater Beck. (*About 35–40 minutes.*)

The more adventurous may wish to view the tarn from above by walking the fine ridge which extends due west between Riggindale and Blea Water, to join High Street above Bleawater Crags. Note the small, unnamed tarn at Caspel Gate. Returning over Mardale

Blea Water The finest and deepest of all Lakeland's corrie tarns broods in its circular amphitheatre.

Ill Bell and descending via Nan Bield Pass brings the added bonus of Small Water – two tarns for the price of one walk. (*About 3–4 hours.*) **See Walk 8.**

SMALL WATER

Grid reference: 455100	Altitude: 452m (1,483ft)	Depth: 16m (52½ft)

A superb little corrie tarn of character this, not as overpowering as its near neighbour and made accessible by the Nan Bield Pass, an ancient track which skirts its northern and western margin. Slab-roofed stone shelters beside the tarn indicate that the track used to be a regular route between Mardale and Kentmere. A. Wainwright speculates on their spidery interiors but one would no doubt overcome such scruples in stormy conditions.

The path from Mardale Head to the tarn and Nan Bield Pass is

Small Water   The view from the head of the Nan Bield Pass.

clearly signposted. The broad track climbs steadily, then narrows as it steepens, with Small Water Beck on the right. Over the final rise the tarn comes into view and stepping stones ease the crossing of the beck. Just beyond the crossing, and to the right of the path, are the shelters. Across the tarn is the tumbling white water of one of the two main inflowing streams; to the right of it, the pass angles upwards.

Like Blea Water, it harbours small brown trout and perch. There is also a greater variety of plant life, mainly consisting of submerged plants, including water lobelia. (*Allow 30 minutes.*) **See Walk 8**.

LITTLEWATER

Grid reference: 509170	Altitude: 255m (837ft)	Depth: 3.5m (11½ft)

This tarn on the eastern fringe of the fells, and 1km (½ mile) north-east of Haweswater Dam, is on private property and there is no public right of way to it. However it can be clearly seen from the public footpath which strikes west-south-west from just west of the farm road serving Littlewater farms, or indeed from the farm road itself. From here it can be viewed in its lowland setting, backed by rounded, green and lightly wooded grassy hillocks. Mature ash and oak trees thinly edge the tarn and a swathe of common reed borders its northern shore. In summer, water lilies display their blooms, while trout, perch and pike lurk beneath the surface. A short stream flows in from the west and another out to the north.

Follow the road to Haweswater; beyond Bampton is Walmgate Foot where a steep, narrow road right (or west) from the cross can be followed to where a private track to Littlewater Hamlet is signed on the left. You should find parking before reaching this turning.

FOUR STONES TARN

Grid reference: 491164	Altitude: 396m (1,300ft)	Depth: 0.5m (1½ft)

It was pure chance that brought me to this little pond, shown but unnamed on the Ordnance Survey map. After a visit to Littlewater I was walking by field paths in the area – to make a day of it – and met a friendly farmer for a 'crack' about the weather, sheep and sundry things – such as tarns! 'Have you been to Fair-st'ns?' he asked.

Later in the year, on a bright but hazy November day, I visited this pond which lies on a little col above the north-western shore of Haweswater and in the shadow of Four Stones Hill. Although shallow, it was encircled by a line of detritus indicating a recent flood level nearly 1m (3ft) above its norm. A dry, rush-choked trench marked its periodic south-western outflow. Rush and starwort seemed to be the principal forms of vegetation; I would guess that the tarn probably dries to marsh during severe drought. A few paces to the east is a circular shelter marked as a cairn on the map, perhaps based on an ancient hut circle. A similar distance west is a pair of standing stones.

Access is by way of the public footpath which starts near the farm road used to see Littlewater Tarn. Continue along this field path to High Drybarrows Farm, pass through the muddy yard and out on to the moor, then follow the broad track which crosses the ford and continues uphill until a prominent left-hand fork leads off to the cairn and tarn.

No expedition here is complete without a visit to Measand Beck, 1km (½ mile) to the south-west. Descend along the path beyond the tarn to gain the prominent foot-bridge over the beck and follow it down on its right-hand side to enjoy its multiple falls. Cross the bridge at the bottom and head back along the shore of Haweswater towards the dam. At the masts on the hill above, take the rising left-hand path to head for Aika Hill, Drybarrows Farm and the outward path.

(From Littlewater to Drybarrows Farm, allow 35 minutes; from Drybarrows to Four Stones Tarn, about 20–30 minutes. From Four Stones to Drybarrows via Measand Beck, allow 1–1½ hours.)

ROUGH HILL TARN

Grid reference: 495194	Altitude: 316m (1,036ft)	Depth: 0.5m (1½ft)

Like most small tarns this is a shy little pond which could easily be passed unnoticed, except for the fact that it is clearly named on the Ordnance Survey map. It stands beside the unfenced road that runs through Heltondale, just south-west of Helton, at a point where a cattle grid and walls divide the rough grazing of the open moorland to the north from the walled pastures of the Butterwick–Bampton area to the south-east. A red postbox in the wall beside the road provides a useful landmark.

The pond is shallow and drains the marsh to the west, its elongated surface hidden by a dense growth of spiky rush. Its bed is of light-brown clay; bladderwort appears to be its principal vegetation. There is little movement of water through the tarn and, when visited, its outflow to the north was partially dry.

HABER TARN

Grid reference: 502225	Altitude: 310m (1,017ft)	Depth: 0.5m (1½ft)

Like Rough Hill Tarn to the south, this is an insignificant little pond located about 1km (½ mile) north-west of Helton village. It is situated in private woodland called Mirebank Plantation.

A long-neglected L-shaped water, it is partially overgrown with weed and surrounded by conifers.

The drift-covered limestone of Askham Fell where this tarn is situated is dotted with sink or shake holes and small, unnamed ponds. The area is crossed by several bridleways, including High Street, the Roman road. Access to Askham Fell can be gained from Pooley Bridge, Askham or Helton.

HASKEW TARN

Grid reference: 522113	Altitude: 468m (1,536ft)	Depth: 1m (3ft)

Sunshine makes all tarns delightful. In rain and mist this would be a wretched place, but with a bright May sun and snowball clouds Haskew Tarn was in buoyant mood. In its peaty bay whirligig beetles whirled; delicate straps of grassy pondweed lay upon the surface, while bog pondweed choked the slow inflow channels which drain the surrounding peat bog. Ten minutes to the east the cairn on Seat Robert points to the sky, while Willy Winder Hill stands guard to the north.

A deep V-cut outflow channel, now clad in peat, indicates that there was a strong outflow in late- or post-glacial times – perhaps from melting ice held in the Haskew basin – before the present peat surface formed. The tarn which now occupies the space in the eroded peat is of comparatively recent formation, and there is some evidence that the western shore, at least, was once wooded.

The tarn may be approached from Truss Gap Farm in the Swindale Valley (with parking just beyond the filter house). A well-marked track leads from the foot-bridge up the fellside – from there you are on your own. It's best to follow Haskew Beck to its source, but choose dry weather. Alternatively you could park at Wet Sleddale Reservoir and climb the fellside to make for Seat Robert, from where the tarn may be seen. (*About 1–1½ hours from Truss Gap Farm.*)

SCALEBARROW TARN

Grid reference: 519152	Altitude: 331m (1,086ft)	Depth: Nil

Although clearly marked and named on the Ordnance Survey map I could find only a weed-choked 'boggy patch' at this location, one of several on Scalebarrow Knott. The walk is pleasant enough but I do not recommend the tarn.

The Tarns
of North-West
Lakeland

The north-west region is the area that lies south of the A66 and west of St John's Vale and the A591, and includes the highland between the valleys of Thirlmere, Borrowdale, Buttermere and Ennerdale. Further west the land declines to the Solway Plain. A line drawn from Castlerigg, through Keswick, to the head of Buttermere, then to Ennerdale, roughly divides the Skiddaw Slates to the north-west from the Borrowdale Volcanic Group to the south-east. Later intrusions of igneous rock occur here within the Skiddaw Slates.

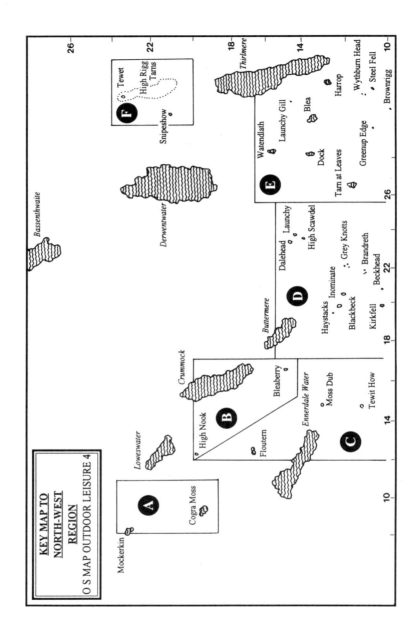

Area A

The first two tarns lie among the declining folds of the Lakeland fells as they merge into the Solway Plain. Mockerkin lies just outside the National Park but is too good to omit.

MOCKERKIN TARN

Grid reference: 083232	Altitude: 115m (377ft)	Depth: 3.5m (11½ft)

The great beauty of Mockerkin is its wonderful summer display of white and yellow water lilies which stretch in broad bands across the south-western corner of the tarn. It is situated some 8km (5 miles) south of Cockermouth, beside the A5086 and between the villages of Mockerkin and Ullock, in gently rolling country just outside the National Park boundary. It occupies a shallow basin surrounded by lush pasture, but along its southern edge curls a steep embankment of glacial origin. A stream, which looks too small to sustain this substantial water, enters from the east beside a

Mockerkin Tarn   Knock Murton Fell peeps from behind the trees on the left.

wooded area fronted by sedge. The gentle outflow from the north-west eventually joins the River Marron.

The tarn has spawned a host of legends – of a sunken town with church and castle, of bells which peal below the water and of the Celtic King Morken said to be buried nearby. Nevertheless, there is some evidence to suggest that it was indeed the site of an early lake village.

There is ample parking in the two laybys overlooking the water, which contains eel, pike and perch.

COGRA MOSS (Arlecdon Reservoir)

Grid reference: 096196	Altitude: 229m (751ft)	Depth: 9m (29½ft)

Just south of Mockerkin Tarn is Cogra Moss, a mainly artificial water retained by a substantial dam across Lakegill Beck. There is little to catch the interest of the tarn-hunter here but its setting among Forestry Commission pines is pleasant enough. Anglers may be seen, thigh-deep, in pursuit of the brown and rainbow trout with which this water is stocked.

Turn off the A5086 road for Lamplugh and continue to Felldyke where there is a small car park. A pleasant signed bridle path leads to the 'tarn'. (*About 20 minutes.*)

Area B

These two tarns lie in the Buttermere–Loweswater area from where they can most easily be reached. Floutern Tarn really belongs in this group (and can be reached from Buttermere) but it has been included in the Ennerdale area because this provides an easier approach.

HIGH NOOK TARN

Grid reference: 124199	Altitude: 221m (725ft)	Depth: 2m (6½ft)

One of High Nook Tarn's most attractive features is its profusion

High Nook Tarn   Beyond, the old coffin road between Loweswater and St Bees Abbey angles across the slope of Carling Knott.

of flowering bogbean, to be seen at its best in June and July. Then, massed flower spikes of pink-tinged, white waxy blooms are held aloft to create a display of rare beauty. Because of the gently shelving margin on the south side, caused by the natural process of infilling, the zone of bogbean is being overtaken by cotton grass encroaching from the shallows.

The tarn itself is in a partially formed corrie set above and beside High Nook Beck, to which it contributes an intermittent outflow; this escapes through a low earth dam topped by a flagged causeway. The inflow from the south, which is equally intermittent, is by way of a small runner from Black Crag, just behind. Heaton Cooper mentions the presence of small, thin trout but I have failed to see them, despite visiting on many occasions.

This delightful tarn is accessible from car parks at the northwestern end of Loweswater or from that at Maggie's Bridge, at the south-eastern end of the lake. (*Allow 1–1½ hours from Loweswater, or 30 minutes from Maggie's Bridge.*) **See Walk 9**.

BLEABERRY TARN

Grid reference: 166155	Altitude: 494m (1,621ft)	Depth: 5m (16½ft)

... there is a large crater that, from the parched colour of the conical mountains in whose bosom it is formed, appears to have been the focus of a volcano in some distant period when the cones were produced by explosion. At present it is the reservoir of water that feeds the roaring cataract in the descent to Buttermere.

Thus were Bleaberry Tarn and Sourmilk Gill described in Father Thomas West's *Guide to the Lakes in Cumberland, Westmorland and Lancashire*, published in 1778. Nowadays we might detect a few inaccuracies in his description of the forces which wrought this concavity.

This classic corrie – where Chapel Crags, flanked by Red Pike and High Stile, frown down upon the trout-filled waters – is deprived of sun from November to March. One might have expected the tarn to have had companions in the neighbouring combes of Ling and Burtness but, lacking retaining moraine dams, they yield only becks which flow down to the Buttermere Valley.

The shortest approach to Bleaberry Tarn is from Buttermere, where some parking is available. Follow the path to the opposite side of the valley, making sure you take the left-hand branch. Cross the outflow from Buttermere (Lake), then ascend the steep signed path for the tarn – uphill all the way. This path has been laboriously restored by National Trust footpath workers; the ascent is fine but watch your step on the way down. (*About 1–1½ hours.*) Other longer routes may be devised, notably the one via Scale Force and Red Pike, visiting the tarn on the descent.

Area C

Ennerdale is probably the least visited of all Lakeland valleys and in my view it is perhaps the finest; judging by the car registration plates in Bowness Knott car park, you might almost think it was reserved for locals only. Floutern Tarn lies on the Buttermere side of the low pass which links that valley with Ennerdale; the other two are beyond the head of Ennerdale Water on the south side of the valley.

FLOUTERN TARN

Grid reference: 124170	Altitude: 377m (1,237ft)	Depth: 4m (13ft)

This is an enigmatic tarn poised above the abrupt fall to the flat and marshy area of Mosedale Head. The water is long and narrow, squeezed into an elongated basin between the lower rocks of Floutern Crag and moraine on the south side and an immense embankment of chunky boulders to the north. The outflow, from the eastern end of this little hanging valley, cascades down a narrow defile in a series of minor falls.

Parallel with the present outflow, and some 150m (164yds) to the north, is a virtual dry valley which suggests that the tarn once spilled over the moraine cutting this former valley, before finally establishing its present outflow.

Apart from the intrinsic interest of its situation and formation, the tarn has a somewhat grim atmosphere, sunk deep in its hollow. Like Bleaberry, Floutern sees little sun during the winter months, and can perhaps be enjoyed more for its views than for its own sake.

The easiest approach is from Ennerdale Valley via Floutern Pass (the long, indistinct track from Buttermere being wet and boggy except in the driest weather). Start from Whin Farm, 3km (2 miles) east of Ennerdale Bridge at 099166; the path is clearly signposted and a layby is conveniently situated nearby. Walk to the top of the pass with Herdus and Great Borne on your right, and a final gate and stile before the descent.

Incidentally, in his guidebook 7, *The Western Fells*, (Great Borne 4), A. W. indicates a direct ascent to Great Borne across Gill Beck. This is *not* a right of way and has been the cause of some distress to a local farmer. I mention this in order to emphasise that the correct approach should be taken to Floutern Tarn.

To continue, although it may seem easier to move right from the gate for some 50m (55yds) to the little stile which gives access to the land around the tarn, this is not a right of way either. The correct way is to proceed along the track downhill and cross the second fence at the second sheepfold (134173) where one gains the open fell. From here, return in a westerly direction uphill again, following the outflow from the tarn. As well as being correct, this is a more interesting approach to the tarn anyway. (*Allow 1–1½ hours.*)

MOSS DUB

Grid reference: 146137	Altitude: 135m (443ft)	Depth: 1m (3ft)

If Ennerdale is the most beautiful of Cumbria's lakes, its tarns fall far short of this standard. Moss Dub is a shallow pond sitting on a brown mud bed in a hollow beside and a little above the River Liza which flows to the lake. The embankment enclosing it is planted with conifers and covered with tree brashings; on the north shore is a small bird-watchers' hide.

The origin of the tarn is somewhat obscure. It does not appear to be an oxbow, yet there is no reason to think it is artificial either. It appears to support little aquatic vegetation (apart from a scattering of sedge) and is skirted by a public path.

Bowness Knott car park on the north shore of Ennerdale Lake is the best starting point. Follow the lake shore to Irish Bridge and cross to the south side of the valley. Then continue up the valley on the forest road until you reach the tarn. (*About 1 hour from Bowness Knott.*)

TEWIT HOW TARN

Grid reference: 146118	Altitude: 602m (1,976ft)	Depth: 0.5m (1½ft)

Some 450m (1,480ft) and almost directly above Moss Dub is Tewit How Tarn. When I visited in early September the temperature had soared into the eighties and all sensible people were enjoying the cool waters of Ennerdale Lake and the River Liza. Instead of doing likewise, I and a hundred friendly flies ascended and descended paths obstructed by the debris of tree felling, deep heather and tall bracken. Although I comforted myself with the thought that I would probably lose several pounds in weight by the end of the day, the sight of Tewit How Tarn's bright water would have been some recompense for all my effort. Alas, a level sward of sedge – the interstices between the tufts filled with pondweed – and, at one corner, a small patch of bogbean, was all that betrayed the tarn's presence. Perhaps in late winter or early spring, before growth begins, the clear water would reflect the impressive sweep of crags from Haycock to Steeple and on to Pillar?

The ascent by tracks beside Low Beck is both steep and obscure and entails considerable effort. From Moss Dub, you'll need a map and compass to find Tewit How. When descending from Tewit How Tarn, avoid the pecked green line on the Ordnance Survey map which would lead you into the horrors of the descent into Deep Gill. It's better by far to stick to the contours of the descending ridge and its heather, down to Ling Mell and into the forest funnel to meet the 'Nine Becks Path', and so to the valley bottom. This is probably also the least unpleasant ascent. (*About 2–2½ hours.*)

Area D

Honister Pass links the head of Buttermere with Borrowdale and all these tarns are located on the upland extending to the north, to the west and to the south of the car park on Honister Hause. This is not to say that the car park is always the best point of departure, for to some extent it precludes circular walks. Time, energy and parking space will probably be the determining factors in choosing your starting point. The first three tarns are north of Honister, below and to the east of Dale Head.

DALEHEAD TARN (Beckhead Tarn)

Grid reference: 230153	Altitude: 498m (1,634ft)	Depth: 1m (3ft)

One of the most delightful resting places, particularly on a bright sunny day, is Dalehead Tarn. From here, there is a choice of onward routes to suit differing abilities and weather conditions. To the north-east is a path to High Spy and on to Maiden Moor; whereas the steep climb west on to Dale Head offers the alternatives of continuing to Hindscarth or Robinson, or simply

Dalehead Tarn   Some campers prepare for an evening swim. The slopes to the right sweep up to Dale Head.

dropping down to Honister Hause. The steep descent eastwards into Borrowdale, via the disused Rigghead Quarries to Rosthwaite or Grange, is yet another option.

Northwards is the valley of Newlands Beck and this has always been my favoured approach. Starting from Little Town where there is limited parking, the ascent is by way of a well-graded track which follows Newlands Beck (keeping the beck on your right), past the spoilheaps of the Goldscope Mine where lead, copper, some silver – and a little gold some say – were once mined. Go past the climbing hut, then take the left-hand rising track which will lead safely above the falls.

At the col, the tarn is not visible from the beck; it lies above and to the right and its discovery provides a mild sense of satisfaction. Beside the tarn is an old sheep pen of rounded boulders. The water itself, set in a secluded, green, level space, is bounded by rock knolls and moraine mounds. To the west, the steep slopes of Dale Head, guarded by grey outcrops, rise to the unseen summit.

A variety of aquatic plants thrive here, including water horsetail, sedge, and water lobelia and the inevitable bogbean. The outflow escapes eastward, to join the head of Newlands Beck.

The shortest approach is from the head of Honister Pass, as for Launchy and High Scawdel Tarns below. (*From Little Town, allow 1–1½ hours.*) **See Walk 10.**

140

LAUNCHY TARN

Grid reference: 233150	Altitude: 553m (1,815ft)	Depth: 75cm (2½ft)

Launchy Tarn is some 400m (440yds) south-east of Dalehead Tarn and about 55m (180ft) above it. Probably because of overgrazing, the peat in this area has been eroded, leaving pools and residual mounds clothed in heather and moorland grasses. The peat depth varies from greater than 2m (6½ft) to less than 1m (3ft).

The tarn itself, the largest pool in the area, plumbed when brimful, measured between 25cm (10in) and 75cm (2½ft) down to bedrock. This was also the depth of the peat around the perimeter – which I checked with a steel-tipped staff one chilly day in early March. A fence line beheads the north-eastern end of the tarn, suggesting that it has been elongated by wave action influenced by the prevailing south-westerly wind since the erection of the fence. At the opposite end is a substantial growth of bogbean, backed by cotton grass.

The shortest approach to Launchy Tarn is from the summit of Honister where there is a handy car park. Follow the path uphill and northwards towards Dale Head. When the steep gradient eases at the 550m (1,800ft) contour, follow this level to the right until the tarns come into view. An old fence line leads directly to the tarns. (*From Honister, about 40–55 minutes.*) **See Walk 10.**

HIGH SCAWDEL TARN

Grid reference: 232147	Altitude: 549m (1,800ft)	Depth: 70cm (2¼ft)

A further 300m (330yds) south-west of Launchy Tarn along the line of a derelict fence is High Scawdel Tarn, really a pair of tarns linked by a short channel and similar in most respects to its neighbour. I recorded depths of between 50cm (20in) and 70cm (2¼ft) to bedrock here. It also supports a small growth of bogbean.
See Walk 10.

Tarns on Haystacks, Buttermere

Nowhere in Lakeland can present such variety of form and surface in so small a compass as Haystacks. No wonder it was hallowed ground to Alfred Wainwright. His ashes rest here, mingling with the peat and gravel underfoot; on a windowsill in Buttermere Church there is an inscribed plaque in his memory, an unusual honour for a lifelong agnostic.

Haystacks is really a continuation of the Red Pike–High Crag ridge but is separated from it by the cleft of Scarth Gap. It forms a narrow, rocky plateau of outcrops and hollows, its fierce crags and gullys overlooking Warnscale Bottom at the head of Buttermere Valley, with more benign slopes southwards to Ennerdale.

The indentations along its crest have gathered surface water, forming many little tarns or ponds. Their numbers multiply after heavy rain, but only three are identified by name. The largest and most easterly of these is Blackbeck Tarn; placed centrally is Innominate or Loaf Tarn, while right beside the summit is the tiny Haystacks Tarn.

There are two main approaches to the Haystacks ridge from Buttermere. The better route is by the old quarry road which begins next to Gatesgarth cottage. This path takes you easily by the green spread of Warnscale Bottom until it steepens into a broad bouldery track that swings in a great arc before rounding a sharp corner above the ravine of Warnscale Beck. Continue above the ravine until you can easily cross on to Haystacks, keeping an eye open for the track. This may be a less exciting approach but it is safer than the one which crosses Warnscale Beck near its confluence with Black Beck before the quarry road ascent begins.

The alternative is via Scarth Gap, taking the signed track beside Gatesgarth Farm, crossing the flat delta at the head of Buttermere (Lake), and ascending this fine pass to its col. Then follow the rather scrambling climb on your left, to the summit of Haystacks.

Whichever way is chosen, a walk taking in the three tarns makes a glorious round of some 8km (5 miles). (*Allow 2½–4 hours.*)

BLACKBECK TARN

Grid reference: 202128	Altitude: 487m (1,598ft)	Depth: 2.5m (8ft)

This fine elongated water, edged by groins of rock, narrows at its northern extremity and discharges its water through a dramatic gap in the crags to tumble in a series of falls and cascades over 300m (985ft) to Warnscale Bottom. The path crosses this outflow – Black Beck – and from the head of the gully there are airy views

Blackbeck Tarn   The summit of Great Gable behind is just hidden by cloud.

down to Buttermere Valley. At the broad, shallow end, sedge, bogbean and water horsetail abound; while in July water lobelia thrust their flower spikes above the surface.

Not only is this a lovely water, it is also a fine viewpoint. Looking southwards along its length, the great north face of Gable rears darkly.

INNOMINATE TARN (Loaf Tarn)

Grid reference: 197129	Altitude: 525m (1,723ft)	Depth: 2m (6½ft)

Innominate (or unnamed) Tarn is perhaps so called because few ever knew it as Loaf Tarn, or perhaps they did not like this old but rather mundane name. It was once suggested that – being the old man's favourite mountain – it should be called Wainwright's Tarn. But good sense, and pressure from those who knew A. W. better, prevailed and this interesting idea was shelved.

However 'a rose by any other name . . .' and a gem of a tarn it still is, set beside the main track some 350m (380yds) north-west of Blackbeck Tarn. Both these tarns are well worth walking around in order to enjoy fully their varied shorelines and plants, as well as the commanding views they offer. Do not miss the tiny round 'handbasin' of a pond just above Innominate and a few paces to the east.

HAYSTACKS TARN

Grid reference: 194132	Altitude: 595m (1,953ft)	Depth: 0.5m (1½ft)

Beside the short summit ridge surmounted by two cairns is this tiny grass-fringed rock pool. Summit tarns are rare and this one somehow manages to persist except in the driest seasons. On my last visit the nearby summit was dominated by a large, white, matronly ewe; bribed with sandwiches, she would obligingly pose for photos while being fondled by children. Is she still there, I wonder?

The little pond is set beside the path just beyond the summit; continue north-west from here, and the descent to Scarth Gap begins.

——— *Tarns on the Brandreth–Great Gable Ridge* ———

From Honister Hause a ridge extends southwards to Great Gable via Grey Knotts and Brandreth where two groups of ponds may be visited; an extension westwards to Kirk Fell will provide two more.

GREY KNOTTS TARNS

Grid reference: 218125	Altitude: 681m (2,235ft)	Depth: 1m (3ft)

Four small tarns are grouped a few paces south of Grey Knotts' summit. They are all peat bog tarns, the largest and deepest being the most southerly. On a clear day one may look westwards along its length and see the distant summit of Pillar. The smallest tarn of the group, which lies on this line of sight, supports a growth of bogbean – the only one of the four to do so.

The usual approach to Grey Knotts from Honister Hause is by way of the repaired path west from the quarry buildings. After a few zigzags up the initial steep ascent, the path joins the track of the old tramway to the ruins of the drum house where the Gable track branches away southwards. After about 500m (550yds), strike south-eastwards over grass to Grey Knotts' summit. (*About 1 hour from the car park on Honister Hause.*)

BRANDRETH TARNS (Three Tarns)

Grid reference: 215115	Altitude: 655m (2,150ft)	Depth: 1m (3ft)

Despite the alternative name, there are actually four tarns here on the col between Brandreth and Green Gable – or perhaps five if one includes the sedge-choked puddle. They provide a pleasant stopping place for those passing to and from Gable on hot summer days.

The most southerly is the largest and deepest; all are fringed by mountain grasses which conceal the underlying peat. One, the most easterly, sustains a growth of bogbean.

From Grey Knotts Tarns, a narrow track leads south-westwards, taking you directly to Brandreth summit. A descent due south over the bouldery terrain then brings you to within sight of Brandreth Tarns. (*From Grey Knotts, about 40 minutes.*)

BECKHEAD TARN

Grid reference: 205107	Altitude: 623m (2,044ft)	Depth: 1m (3ft)

On the col known as Beck Head, between Gable and Kirk Fell, are two small tarns, one intermittent, the other larger and holding water all year round. Like most col tarns, it is wave-stretched at right angles to the ridge on which it lies. Black peaty mud and submerged flags form the bottom of this clear, shallow tarn which appears to have neither inlet nor outlet.

From Brandreth Tarns, descend about 30m (100ft) west or south-west down easy slopes to gain Moses Trod near the head of Tongue Beck. The distinct track should then be followed below the daunting crags on the north face of Gable, to gain that fell's north-western ridge. From here a magnificent view down the length of Wastwater and its valley can be enjoyed. More directly below, in the col, is Beckhead Tarn. (*From Brandreth Tarns, perhaps 45 minutes.*)

KIRKFELL TARN

Grid reference: 197106	Altitude: 752m (2,466ft)	Depth: 1m (3ft)

Kirk Fell consists of two summits. Between them is a broad, flat saddle on which lie two tarns: one smaller, shallower and irregular

Kirkfell Tarn   The rocky dome of Great Gable looms from behind Kirkfell.

in shape; the other deeper and elongated. There is no surface connection between them, although they are within a few metres of each other. A boulder fringe runs parallel with the western edge of the larger tarn which contains clear water but has a black peaty bottom. At the time of my visit in early May its smaller companion sustained a dense growth of bright green algae.

From these turf-edged tarns one can enjoy a spectacular view of Gable with its bald, rounded summit and steep northern and southern faces in profile.

To reach the tarns, take the steep bouldery ascent from the Beck Head col to Kirk Fell's first and lower summit. The tarns lie side by side on the saddle below. (*From Beck Head, allow 40 minutes.*)

The best return route to Honister is by way of Moses Trod which passes below the north face of Great Gable and continues to Brin Crags. At the line of boundary posts, incline right to pick up the track to the drum house and the descent to Honister Hause. (*Allow 1½–2 hours from Kirk Fell to Honister Hause.*)

Area E

South of Keswick, a broad ridge of high moorland extends from north to south between Thirlmere in the east and Borrowdale in the west. The streams of importance which drain this ridge are Launchy Gill and Wyth Burn on the eastern side towards Thirlmere; to the west into Borrowdale flow Watendlath Beck and Stonethwaite Beck, the latter resulting from the confluence of Greenup Gill and Langstrath Beck. Within this area are ten named tarns and groups of tarns, the best-known of which is probably Watendlath Tarn. For 'technical reasons' I also have to include in this area Tarn at Leaves on Rosthwaite Fell, which is really an extension of the Allen Crags–Glaramara ridge.

WATENDLATH TARN

Grid reference: 276162	Altitude: 263m (863ft)	Depth: 17m (56ft)

Hugh Walpole selected this fine, secluded tarn and the ancient farmsteads which stand at its foot as the fictional home of Judith Paris in his haunting *Herries* saga. The small area of level pasture that surrounds the water, together with the sheep runs on the surrounding fellsides, was sufficient to provide a bare livelihood in earlier times. Nowadays tourism provides an essential addition to income, as does fish farming. (The tarn is stocked with brown and rainbow trout by Borrowdale Fisheries.) Probably owing to its sheltered situation, it contains a wide variety of aquatic plants, including white and yellow water lilies.

Geomorphologically speaking, this tarn stands at the head of a hanging valley; after flowing some 3km (2 miles) northwards, Watendlath Beck descends with a flourish in the form of Lodore Falls, to lose itself in Derwentwater.

Access to the tarn is easy except on high days and holidays. The single-track road leading to the hamlet branches off the Borrowdale Road near the head of Derwentwater. There is limited parking on the way and at Watendlath itself.

147

BLEA TARN, ARMBOTH

Grid reference: 292141	Altitude: 476m (1,562ft)	Depth: 13m (43ft)

Bleatarn Gill, the major contributor of water to Watendlath Tarn, finds its source in Blea Tarn, one of three so named in Lakeland. Gentle slopes of coarse grass surround this natural tarn situated in a shallow concavity at the mid-point of this broad ridge of peaty moorland. The crags of Coldbarrow Fell stand well back and do not overshadow the water; still further south is the Norse-sounding Ullscarf on whose lower slopes the main inflowing streams originate. The northern outflow winds between low ridges and across peaty marsh, plunges steeply into a narrow ravine and finally idles through the fields at the head of Watendlath before mingling its waters with the tarn.

To reach Blea Tarn, take the path from the hamlet which ascends the steep fellside behind and to the east of the farms and car park. When the slope eases, take the southern branch and plod over 2.5km (1½ miles) of gentle but boggy tracks to the tarn. The water contains a wide selection of plants, including yellow water lilies. (*Allow 1½ hours.*)

From here, you can continue past the tarn in a south-easterly direction to the top of the ridge, then descend by clear, drier tracks to Harrop Tarn and Thirlmere.

HARROP TARN

Grid reference: 312136	Altitude: 304m (997ft)	Depth: 5m (16½ft)

Tarn Crag rears up behind Harrop, giving the impression that this is a corrie tarn, though much reduced in surface area and depth by the deposition of sediment. The surrounding marshland has been planted with conifers, while the extent of its shallows is indicated by the large, encroaching beds of sedge, water horsetail and yellow water lily.

Like Blea, much of Harrop Tarn's water originates from the Ullscarf catchment area. Attractive falls and cascades occur in Dod Gill, the present discharge from the tarn, but the presence of a deep, dry valley, partly utilised by the approach path a few paces to the north and parallel to the gill, suggests that this was once an alternative outfall.

148

Being easily accessible, this tarn is popular with visitors. There are car parks and toilet facilities at Dobgill Bridge and little effort is required to negotiate the 500m (550yds) of steep path.

In the surrounding Forestry Commission plantations there are waymarked paths, but the more energetic may wish to continue along the track which skirts the northern shore and leads to the western boundary fence. This takes you over the moor to Blea Tarn and Watendlath. (*Allow 20–40 minutes from Dobgill Bridge to Harrop Tarn. From Harrop Tarn to Blea Tarn, allow 45 minutes.*)

LAUNCHY GILL TARN

Grid reference: 302150	Altitude: 385m (1,263ft)	Depth: 1m (3ft)

The Ordnance Survey map fails to include the word 'Gill' in the name of this tarn. This omission makes it rather difficult to differentiate between this and the other Launchy Tarn on High Scawdel, which by sheer coincidence lies on the same Northings grid line 15 but further to the west.

The tarn is a circular swelling, some 6m (20ft) in diameter, in Launchy Gill. Water slides in across a gently sloping band of rock, pauses a while, then slowly exits on either side of a small grassy island just before the outflow.

Heather and coarse grasses clothe the level moorland here; I watched while a dragonfly busied herself laying eggs at the pond margin. No paths lead to this secret cistern. If you too should wish to savour its solitude, strike north from where the Blea Tarn path leaves the Harrop forest boundary and follow the fence north to Stone Hause. Pass between the crags into the marshy zone, then follow the drainage to Launchy Gill. (*About 30 minutes.*)

DOCK TARN

Grid reference: 274144	Altitude: 403m (1,323ft)	Depth: 5m (16½ft)

I hold Dock Tarn in special regard because it is the first tarn I really saw as an object of beauty and enduring interest. When I first set out in search of it a number of years ago, the track from Watendlath tended to lose itself in marshland. More recently, the path has been waymarked, becoming more distinct with usage.

Dock Tarn This shy tarn hides amongst the knolls and crags of Watendlath Fell. A view looking south.

Concealed within a shallow valley, with its island, promontories and bays, the tarn presents a wonderfully varied shoreline, with steep bare rocks to the west, and bouldery, heather-clad slopes to the east. I like it best in winter when the wavelets are stilled by the sealing ice which, crumpled at the rim, reflects the angled sun.

Considering its altitude, Dock Tarn is particularly well-favoured in its range of plant life. According to Stokoe, the common reed (usually a denizen of richer, lowland waters) finds a place here; as does the small white water lily – surely its highest occurrence in Lakeland.

One approach is from Watendlath, but make sure you take the lower path beside that tarn or you will end up at Rosthwaite. (*Allow 1 hour from Watendlath.*) The alternative, steeper approach is from Stonethwaite. Turn right after crossing Stonethwaite Bridge, then take the rising repaired path beside Willy-grass Gill, the outflow from Dock Tarn. (*About 1–1½ hours.*)

It's possible to traverse between Dock and Blea Tarn, but there are no paths across the intervening wet, peaty moor, so a compass is essential.

——— *Tarns in the Greenup Edge–Wyth Burn Area* ———

To the south of the foregoing larger tarns is a scattering of small fry which may be netted in a single expedition by the reasonably competent, energetic walker in possession of a map and compass.

One of the beauties of tarn-hunting is that it leads one across unfamiliar country which the peak-bagger might neglect. In this case the tarns in question are Greenup Edge Tarn, Brownrigg Tarn, Steel Fell Tarn and the Wythburn Head Tarns. One may visit them singly or in any combination and from whatever direction one chooses. However my chosen round includes them all and has the advantage of good parking facilities. (*Allow about 4–5 hours in all.*)

The start is from the car park at Dobgill Bridge beside Thirlmere, as for Harrop Tarn, and the first leg is to Harrop itself.

GREENUP EDGE TARNS

Grid reference: 289110	Altitude: 622m (2,041ft)	Depth: 0.5m (1½ft)

Many anonymous ponds are scattered upon this grassy ridge, some permanent, others appearing in wet weather and deceptively similar to the ones we seek. But Greenup Edge Tarns, the largest hereabouts, lie just over 500m (550yds) north of the col where the Greenup Gill–Easedale track crosses Greenup Edge. The ridge is broad and level, dotted with grey boulders and grey sheep around the two shallow tarns. Little rock knolls occur nearby, the largest topped with a small cairn.

There is nothing spectacular about these ponds, for they yield little beyond a sparse growth of sedge. From this viewpoint, the next two tarns, Brownrigg and Steel Fell, can both be seen eastwards across the Wyth Burn valley.

To reach Greenup Edge from Harrop Tarn, cross Dobgill by the stepping stones at the outflow to gain Ullscarf Gill, the main inflow. Follow this interesting stream and, where it divides, take the south-western branch that goes past the sheepfold and towards Black Knott. Continue south-westwards over steadily rising rough grassland until you reach the ridge path. Then follow the ridge path in a southerly direction to find the tarns. (*Allow 1½–2 hours.*)

BROWNRIGG TARN

Grid reference: 297105	Altitude: 495m (1,624ft)	Depth: 1m (3ft)

From Greenup Edge Tarns, head south for the col and take the Easedale track. Before it descends, swing left to head for Calf Crag. Brownrigg Tarn will appear below, on the left.

This tarn, sunk in the peat amid mounds of moraine, is substantially larger than the previous ones – and was once larger still, judging by the marshy terrain that extends beyond its present shoreline. I found it alive with jewel-like whirligig beetles, overseen by a pair of dragonflies. Sedge and some reluctant bogbean grow here. (*From Greenup Edge Tarns, allow 1 hour.*)

STEEL FELL TARN (Rough Crag Tarn)

Grid reference: 308112	Altitude: 468m (1,536ft)	Depth: 1m (3ft)

All tarns reflect the weather in their moods, so it is unfortunate that every time I have passed here the sky has been overcast. Steel Fell is permanent and larger than Brownrigg and perhaps offers more of interest than my impressions have led me to believe. In summer, bogbean and sedge abound, and the fluffy heads of cotton grass nod about the rim. A smaller, similar pond exists beyond; further still, the ridge rises in a series of rocky humps towards the summit of Steel Fell.

From Brownrigg Tarn, a line of old fenceposts extends north-westwards along the ridge to Steel Fell Tarn. (*About 20 minutes.*)

WYTHBURN HEAD TARNS

Grid reference: 305115	Altitude: 405m (1,329ft)	Depth: 1.5m (5ft)

From Steel Fell Tarn, head downhill (a little west of north), following the easier slopes into the Wyth Burn Valley. As you descend, the flat marshy area known as The Bog, the site of some former tarn, can be seen to the left. Ahead, where a group of moraines on the valley floor has partially blocked its path, the burn swells into a string of three larger and two smaller pools. Their stillness, depth and vegetation give them a tarn-like character, for they support white water lily, spike rush and water horsetail.

To complete this round, follow the path downstream, past three delightful waterfalls, until you reach the road at Stockhow Bridge. About 1.5km (1 mile) northwards along the road is Dobgill Bridge car park. (*From Steel Fell Tarn to Wythburn Head Tarns, allow 15 minutes; from Wythburn Head Tarns to Stockhow Bridge, about 30–45 minutes.*)

TARN AT LEAVES

Grid reference: 258122	Altitude: 499m (1,638ft)	Depth: 5m (16½ft)

I have been unable to establish any reason for this unusual name but it certainly lends an air of enchantment to this little tarn. I found it an appealing water, snug on a shelf above Langstrath and protected at its back by a small crag bearing a stunted rowan tree. Along its eastern margin grows a forest of water horsetail, which merges into sedge and then bur-reed. Near the outfall the rock margin drops sheer; here, 2m (6½ft) down, the tarn bed glows red in sunlight. The slow outflow moves marshily towards the lip of the shelf before plunging down, as Tansey Gill, to Langstrath Beck. Looking south-east from just above the tarn, the long ridge of Greenup Edge and High Raise appears to culminate in the hump of Pike of Stickle.

Having parked at Seatoller, the easiest approach is by way of Combe Gill. From the fell gate, strike up the eastern flank of the combe, angling right to pick up a faint track, later reinforced by small cairns. Keeping well clear of Rottenstone Gill on your right (its name is a literal description), make for the low point or col in the ridge above. Once over the col, the tarn is visible just below and beyond. (*From the road by Mountain View Cottages, allow 1 hour.*)

If you wish to make an expedition including Glaramara – and perhaps Allen Crags – walk southwards over Rosthwaite Fell to

Great Hollow where there are several small tarns. Here a faint trod can be picked up, strengthening into a path. Be careful to keep right and follow the path over a small ridge, curving westwards into the broad, marshy col of Combe Head. (It is worth repeating Wainwright's warning that this is dangerous country in mist.) Across the col is the rock bastion of Glaramara. A frontal attack involves scrambling up a weakness in its walls, but its eastern side offers an easier ascent. (*From the tarn, allow 50 minutes.*) From Glaramara, continue southwards to Allen Crags or return by the Combe Gill track.

Area F

These tarns are all within easy walking distance of Keswick and lie on either side of the A591 Keswick–Ambleside road. Snipeshow is at the extreme north-eastern tip of the moorland ridge described in Area E.

SNIPESHOW TARN

Grid reference: 296211	Altitude: 227m (673ft)	Depth: 0.5m (1½ft)

Almost directly behind, and some 70m (230ft) above the house of Brackenrigg, is tiny Snipeshow Tarn. It is held in a secluded, bouldery hollow barely 300m (330yds) from the A591 Keswick to Ambleside road but high above it so that one has the impression of being deep within fell country. An outcrop of grey rock surmounted by an isolated rowan overhangs the tarn, but above and beyond is the great bulk of Dodd Crag.

The pond itself is fairly small, with many scattered angular rocks upon its bed and a large grey boulder standing sentinel. There is no surface inflow or outflow but what appears to be an artificial channel lies at the western end, just above the apparent high water mark. In times of severe flooding this would ensure that surplus water was directed north-westwards, towards Causeway Foot and Naddle Beck. The tarn was reported dry in the

Snipeshow Tarn   A giant boulder presides over this little tarn.

severe drought of 1976; I also found it so in July 1992. On one visit I thought I spied a fish. Instead it turned out to be a palmate newt, several in fact, scrambling over the mud surface between the rocks and water starwort.

Access is by way of a ladder stile on the western side of the A591, midway between Causeway Foot and Brackenrigg. Follow the path behind the copse; and near its end look out for a thin track which angles up and right, eventually passing through a shallow valley to the tarn. The layby at Rough How Bridge is recommended, as sections of footpath provide safer passage beside this busy road. The two-hour time limit at the layby should give you ample time for a visit. (*From the roadside stile, allow 15–20 minutes.*)

—— *Tarns on High and Low Rigg (Naddle Fell)* ——

Just over 3km (2 miles) east of Keswick is a veritable island of moorland – a hummocky ridge – rising to nearly 350m (1,148ft), extending from north to south, and separated from adjacent

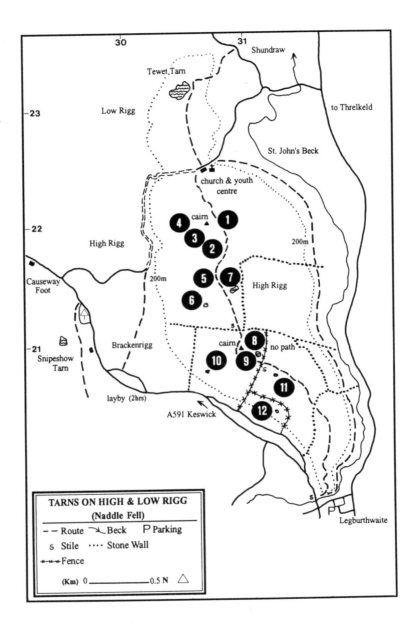

uplands by the valley of St John's Beck, the outflow from Thirlmere and the ancient lakebed of the Naddle Valley, now drained by Naddle Beck. The uneven outline of this ridge is largely due to its rocks having a variable resistance to weathering. Harder andesite lavas alternate with softer tuff (consolidated volcanic ash) in this northern manifestation of the Borrowdale Volcanic Group, resulting in the knobbly texture of Naddle Fell. In contrast, the smoother outlines of Skiddaw reflect the homogeneous nature of the Skiddaw Slates, which have a more uniform resistance to erosion.

Low Rigg, the northern extension of the moorland, is, as its name suggests, lower than High Rigg, from which it is separated by a fault line followed by the lane which links St John's in the Vale with Dale Bottom. On the brow is the Carlisle Diocesan Youth Centre and St John's Church, the latter built to serve the communities on either side of the fell. Low Rigg holds Tewet Tarn, the one tarn of significance on this highland area; the other twelve, all located on High Rigg, are mostly small ephemeral ponds which are reduced to marshy hollows in summer droughts. To the tarn-hunter, this is a magical fell where little ponds play hide and seek around the hummocks and hollows, between ridges and in deep marshy dells. If you go to the cairn above St John's Church and look south you will see three or four nearby. Seek them on the ground and you will soon see what I mean.

The walking is also varied and full of interest. Broad, well-used, grassy paths extend the length of the fell and stiles ease the crossing of walls and fences. Bridleways and footpaths follow the base of the hill on either side, that on the east side between St John's Church and the A591 being the more interesting. To take in the whole fell, it's best to start by the stile beside St John's Beck Bridge, Snaithwaite (on the A591) and climb the uphill track, bearing left at the two earlier forks; see sketch map shown opposite. Cars may be left at the Legburthwaite car park, courtesy of North West Water; the entrance is from the St John's in the Vale road opposite Castle Rock. (*Allow 1½–2 hours to Tewet Tarn, plus as much time as you wish to spend tarn-hunting on High Rigg.*)

These tarns do not have names so I have numbered them from 1 to 12 from the cairned high point at the northern end of the fell.

Looking north from here, Tewet Tarn can be seen. Southwards, 1 to 4 are in view, 4 appearing only in wet weather. These, together with 5, 6 and 10, were sealed by a layer of thin, clear ice on a recent visit, beneath which the vegetation – mainly creeping bent – stood clear and bright as day. However, they lacked etched margins, suggesting that in drier periods they would perhaps retreat to the rush patch each one held.

No. 5 is the highest of all the ponds. From it No. 6 lies south-south-west on an isolated prominence.

No. 7, below and to the east of 5, occupies a low, marshy area. It is shallow, but, having a large catchment area, probably survives all but the driest periods. Testimony to its permanence is the presence of water horsetail and bogbean.

No. 8 hides in a windy gap below the southern cairned summit; again it is a permanent pond with a well-established shoreline and a depth of 1m (3ft). Bogbean and bur-reed grow here.

No. 11 is a reedy pond lying in a marshy hollow below the path.

No. 12 lies on private agricultural land, and is fenced off from the fell. It is very clear and has a depth of 1.5m (5ft), but its squared shape suggests human influence. A ruined sheepfold nearby may mean that it was formerly used for sheep dipping.

TEWET TARN (Tewfit Tarn)

Grid reference: 304236	Altitude: 205m (672ft)	Depth: 2m (6½ft)

Its name is perhaps derived from the peewits which often wheel about this, the largest of the tarns on Naddle Fell. It stands on a sheep-cropped shelf, overlooked by a nearby rock outcrop. A low barrage of turf-bound boulders supports its northern shoreline, where spike rush, water lobelia and some broadleaved pondweed grow in the shallows. Water horsetail abounds, and sedge encroaches around the southern marshy perimeter to provide a haven for coot. The placid water mirrors the bold outline of Blencathra across the Threlkeld valley.

A path almost opposite St John's Church leads to the tarn. But the shortest approach is from the lane just north of Shundraw, where a signed footpath provides access within 15 minutes.

The Outlying Tarns: Northern Region

These six tarns are associated with the Skiddaw–Blencathra block of highland and five of them unfortunately require the Landranger 90 Ordnance Survey map. Bright Tarn is mentioned, even though it lies just outside the National Park boundary; although unnamed on the Landranger map it is identified on the Outdoor Leisure map 5. With the exception of Bright Tarn, which is on Carboniferous Limestone all these waters lie on the Skiddaw Slates.

Bowscale Tarn and particularly Scales Tarn are good examples of corrie tarns, both wholly natural, as is Little Tarn, a lowland water reputed to be bottomless and sustaining an interesting carr development.

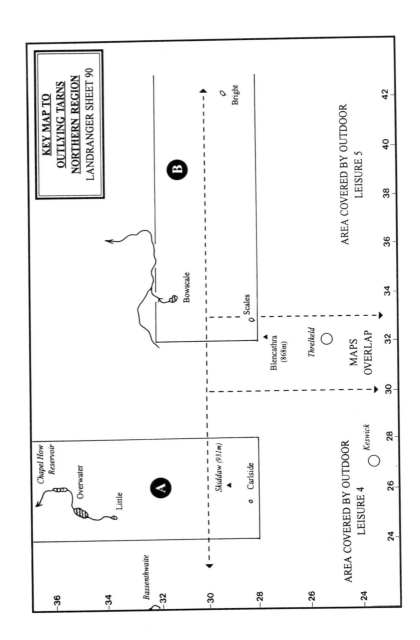

KEY MAP TO
OUTLYING TARNS
NORTHERN REGION
LANDRANGER SHEET 90

Chapel How
Reservoir

Overwater

Little

Bassenthwaite

A

Skiddaw (931m)

o Carlside

AREA COVERED BY OUTDOOR
LEISURE 4

Keswick

Bowscale

B

Bright

Scales

Blencathra
(868m)

Threlkeld

MAPS
OVERLAP

AREA COVERED BY OUTDOOR
LEISURE 5

Area A

These tarns – grouped for convenience of approach, and because they lie in close proximity horizontally if not vertically – are to be found on the western side of the Skiddaw–Blencathra massif. The first two are on the lower ground north-east of Bassenthwaite village and close to Orthwaite. In contrast, little Carlside is high on the fell, 200m (650ft) below and south-west of Skiddaw summit.

LITTLE TARN (Nevin Tarn)

| Grid reference: 249338 | Altitude: 198m (650ft) | Depth: 3.5m (11ft) est. |

North of Bassenthwaite village a narrow watershed extends between Great Cockup in the Skiddaw block and Binsey to the north-west, separating the natural drainage which flows south-wards into Bassenthwaite and the River Derwent from that which flows northwards into the River Ellen via Orthwaite Valley and Chapel House Gorge. In Orthwaite Valley are two named tarns, and one reservoir which I have ignored.

Little Tarn The enriched water of this lowland tarn is surrounded by willow carr. The valley of Dash Beck lies beyond.

From the road that runs through the hamlet of Orthwaite, Little Tarn can be seen in the valley below, enshrouded by trees. Just north of the farm a stone stile sets you on a footpath extending north-westwards towards Overwater Hall. Beyond the first gateway, take the left-hand branch running south-westwards towards Bassenthwaite village. After crossing the outflow of the tarn, follow the indistinct path left and uphill to gain an excellent view of the water.

This typical lowland tarn, with its sheltered site and enriched water, supports an abundance of aquatic plants which provide a classic example of zoning. At the northern outflow end of this oval water, lilies – white and yellow – are succeeded landwards by bogbean, club rush, common reed, then carr of willow and birch. At the southern end, where two lazy streams enter, the club rush and reed are absent; otherwise the zoning is similar. On the two longer sides, the distribution of plants is more haphazard and the carr is thinner. Pike, perch and eels reside here, though the fishing is private. The tarn is said to be bottomless, but I suspect it is no deeper than Skelsmergh which has been similarly described; the term really refers to the lack of a firm bed. (*From Orthwaite, allow 10–15 minutes.*) **See Walk 11.**

OVERWATER

Grid reference: 252350	Altitude: 188m (617ft)	Depth: 18m (59ft) est.

Overwater may well have looked something like Little Tarn before a low dam was built at its northern outflow, raising the level sufficiently to kill the bordering trees and make the former boathouse untenable. This was done some time in the 1920s to provide water for Wigton. Except on the steeper western side, it is edged by gentle fields and lies open to the skies. Indeed it would appear bland and characterless, were it not for the distant frieze of the Skiddaw fells.

The water supports a wide range of plants, from lilies white and yellow to water lobelia, but as there is no public access to the shore these must bloom in obscurity. The road from Orthwaite passes close enough, along three sides in fact, but the best view may be had from the road to Uldale. From here one can look down upon the whole tarn and beyond to Skiddaw.

CARLSIDE TARN

Grid reference: 256283	Altitude: 715m (2,346ft)	Depth: 0.5m (1½ft)

This tiny tarn, some 12m × 3m (39ft × 10ft) in area, has the distinction of being the only ridge or col tarn on the Skiddaw Slates. It lies on the col between Skiddaw summit and Carlside (a windy gap that keeps the muddy water almost constantly in motion), and appears to be eroding under the influence of wave action mainly at the south-eastern end. Apart from providing sky-bright reflections in this bleak, slaty environment, it has little intrinsic merit and has a habit of drying out in summer when its presence would be most appreciated. The constant water motion and the ephemeral nature of the tarn ensure that no plants grow here.

The steep path descending south-westwards from Skiddaw summit passes the tarn, which is shown and named on the Outdoor Leisure 4 Ordnance Survey map but not on the Landranger 90.

The ascent of Skiddaw by the tourist route from Keswick via Latrigg is dull, eroded and crowded in summer. My favoured approach is from the northern side, starting from Peter House Farm on the Orthwaite road and following the bridle track to Skiddaw House as far as Whitewater Dash. From the head of the falls, follow the old fence line south-westwards up the fellside to Bakestall; then continue upwards, aiming for the highest point ahead, to arrive at the summit ridge. After descending to Carlside Tarn, curve westwards, then north-westwards along Longside Edge to Ullock Pike, finally descending to the Orthwaite road north of High Side. Parking is available in small laybys along the road. (*Allow 4–5 hours.*)

Area B

The upland tarns of Scales and Bowscale lie to the west and north of Blencathra respectively. Little Bright Tarn is on the lower, undulating ground to the east of the highland block, close to Greystoke; it has more in common with the Orthwaite tarns, though it lacks their attractive setting.

SCALES TARN

Grid reference: 329282	Altitude: 595m (1,953ft)	Depth: 8m (26ft)

Much like a smaller-scale Blea Water, Scales Tarn is an almost circular water sunk within a deep corrie on the eastern slopes of Blencathra. It is flanked to the north by the superb arête, Sharp Edge, which affords a thrilling route (dangerous in winter) to the summit of this flat-topped fell.

In wet conditions, steep streams descend the grooved crags at the back of the tarn. They emerge in the form of Scales Beck, joining the Glenderamackin which flows north to Mungrisdale, before doubling back again to enter the Greta.

From the shore, the tarn looks shallow, with many partly submerged boulders, but it soon plunges to 3m (10ft) and then 8m (26ft) near the centre. Plants are scarce; whatever deficiency in the water accounts for this probably also explains the lack of fish.

There are convenient laybys on the A66 near the White Horse Inn, about 2km (1 mile) east of Threlkeld. The back road past the inn leads to Mousthwaite Combe where a prominent path ascends to the lower slopes of Scales Fell. From here, follow the path above the Glenderamackin and then left, up Scales Beck, to the tarn. (*Allow 1–1½ hours.*)

BOWSCALE TARN

Grid reference: 336313	Altitude: 477m (1,565ft)	Depth: 17m (56ft)

Visitors should be warned that this tarn is said to harbour two immortal trout. Legend has it that they are even endowed with the power of speech, but, despite making several visits at different seasons, I have failed to make contact with them. Perhaps, after so many centuries, their solitude began to pall and they slipped away down the steep beck to the River Caldew and so north to Carlisle and the Solway. This desire to escape would be quite understandable, for little of the outside world can be seen from their deep fastness.

Bowscale Tarn   The outflow (foreground) flows to the river Caldew. These waters hold the fabled 'talking fish'.

Behind, to the west and south, rears the great precipice of Tarn Crag, and the circle is completed – apart from the gap through which the outflow passes – by a great whaleback of a moraine. To be constantly gazed upon by a succession of pony-borne Victorians hungry for terrifying sights, or scourged by the hooks of careless anglers, perhaps proved too much even for immortal trout.

From a human viewpoint this is an impressive, moody tarn: oppressive when melting snow clings to the crags and dull clouds hang overhead; lonely when grey winds curl downwards, sending rippling cats' paws chasing back across the surface, and the rush of descending water echoes from the gullies. Then again, in bright summer, it can be a sheltered, peaceful place, the sunlight twinkling on its dappled surface.

Shoreweed and water lobelia grow here. The pony track from Bowscale hamlet, between Mungrisdale and Mosedale, is an easy stroll. (*Allow 45 minutes–1 hour.*)

BRIGHT TARN (Berrier End Tarn)

Grid reference: 421294	Altitude: 275m (902ft)	Depth: 5m (16½ft)

This tarn lies on private agricultural land but can be viewed through a wide gap in the wall next to the road. It lies just outside the National Park boundary but I mention it here because of its interesting situation.

The country rock hereabouts is Carboniferous Limestone, overlain with fine glacial drift consisting mainly of red-brown clay. This limestone is noted for its permeability, surface water tending to disappear underground by way of swallow holes. Indeed there is a line of such depressions parallel to the southern side of the tarn and some 25m (27yds) from it. Another swallow hole 4.5m (15ft) in depth, its lip barely a pace from the tarn's boulder-reinforced edge, accepts the outfall.

Heaton Cooper says this swallow hole was deliberately dug by some former Lord of Greystoke in order to reduce the marshland beyond the tarn – the other four holes being earlier abortive attempts to unlock the drainage. Its former outflow westwards was blocked by a rock and sod dam, he suggests (though I saw no sign of this), but the full tarn certainly brimmed over in that direction where much rush-covered marshland exists. There is no surface inflow, so groundwater probably drains in from the surrounding undulating moorland.

The tarn lies on the back road between Berrier End and Greystoke, about 2.5km (1¼ miles) south-west of Greystoke.

The Outlying Tarns: Southern Region

The Ordnance Survey Outdoor Leisure maps 6 and 7 extend southwards to grid line Northing 90; however a number of important tarns lie south of this, in the same latitude as the southern ends of Lakes Coniston and Windermere. For these it is necessary to consult Landranger 96. Area A includes the tarns west of Coniston; Area B, those between Coniston and Windermere; and Area C, those east of Windermere. The A593 road between Coniston and Broughton-in-Furness roughly follows the boundary between the Borrowdale Volcanic Group rocks which lie to the north-west of it and the Silurian Slates to the south-east, on which these 'outlying tarns' are situated. The fells here consist of low, undulating ridges declining southwards towards Morecambe Bay. From various elevated view-points one can see across the bay towards Fleetwood and the Fylde Coast.

Many of the tarns in this area were originally created for sporting or amenity purposes and are on private ground. They also become progressively less characteristic of tarns as one moves south. I have therefore ignored the few other so-called tarns outside the southern boundary of the National Park.

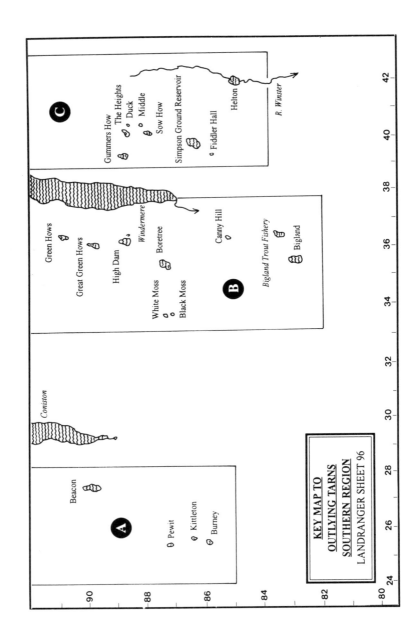

A

Beacon

Pewit
Kittleton
Burney

Coniston

Green Hows

Great Green Hows

High Dam

Windermere

White Moss
Black Moss
Boretree

B

Canny Hill

Bigland Trout Fishery

Bigland

C

Gummers How
The Heights
Duck
Middle
Sow How

Simpson Ground Reservoir

Fiddler Hall

Helton

R. Winster

**KEY MAP TO
OUTLYING TARNS
SOUTHERN REGION
LANDRANGER SHEET 96**

80 82 84 86 88 90

24 26 28 30 32 34 36 38 40 42

Area A

This is 'brown country', or that is my impression when I compare it with Area B. It mainly consists of bracken and heather moorland, their brown and dun tones predominating in winter. The area has few trees, bristles with fingerposts and is interlaced with footpaths.

BEACON TARN

Grid reference: 274901	Altitude: 163m (535ft)	Depth: 8m (26ft)

What a pity this fine tarn is partly cut off the Outdoor Leisure 6 map, for it should really be visited at the same time as Torver Tarn, the two being conveniently linked by the Cumbria Way. Alternatively, parking may be found midway between Lake Bank and Brown How, beside the A5084, on the western side of Coniston. A broad track, not shown on the Ordnance Survey map, quickly

Beacon Tarn The rich purple of the heather-clad moraines and the distant Coniston fells create a magical setting in late summer.

leads from here to the tarn. Another, longer route is from Water Yeat via Greenholme Farm.

The tarn itself is a superb natural feature situated in a broad basin flanked by low fells. From its southern end, Coniston Old Man, Dow Crag and Walna Scar can be seen away to the north. Moraine hummocks at the southern end form a natural dam so that the outflowing stream is deflected eastwards. Its shallow water flows over a bed of shale to curl around the moraine and away beside the path to Water Yeat.

There is a fine selection of aquatic plants here, including most of those described in the introduction to this book. The southern, western and northern margins, crossed by several inflowing streams, are marshy; while the eastern edge is steep and rocky. In summer the tarn is a popular picnic place and an ideal place to swim and sunbathe, well away from the crowds on Coniston's shores. One elderly visitor asked me, as I stood gazing at the water, if there were any fish in it. I said I thought there were brown trout; I can now add pike and perch to the list. (*About 40 minutes by the broad track from the A5084. Between Torver and Beacon Tarns, allow 1 hour.*)

BURNEY TARN, KITTLETON TARN and PEWIT TARN (Heathwaite Tarn)

Grid reference: 254859	Altitude: 149m (489ft)	Depth: 2m (6½ft)

Midway between Lowick Green and Grizebeck on the A5092 (which forms the southern boundary of the National Park hereabouts), Great Burney is a prominent feature on the northern side of the road. About 1km (½ mile) west of Gawthwaite, an unfenced minor road branches off and skirts the western side of the fell. A further 1km (½ mile) along this road a flat area of marsh comes into view on the left, with the tarn a short distance away, surrounded in summer by a thicket of reeds.

Walking across the marsh is difficult except in the driest weather but a low ridge extends across the wetland just to the north, permitting a drier approach, though the tarn is still some 50m (55yds) away. From here I was able to see a zone of lily pads within the encircling reeds; the centre was clear water. My September visit raised some 30 pairs of mallard who departed noisily.

Some 300m (330yds) further along, on the right-hand side of the road, is Kittleton Tarn (256862), a small, shallow pond of no great character.

Nearly 1km (½ mile) on, a left-hand turning passes close to Pewit or Heathwaite Tarn (253873), similar to but a little larger than Kittleton Tarn.

Area B

In contrast to Area A, this is 'green country', full of rich pastures and abundant woodland. Foothpaths are not so numerous, as the land is more intensively farmed, and those that are there appear to be rarely used. This is gentle walking country, with much grazing land, and dogs should be kept under control.

GREEN HOWS (High Tarn) and GREAT GREEN HOWS

Grid reference: 362907/360899   Altitudes: 150m (492ft)/186m (610ft)   Depth:?

Both these waters are artificial and lie on the private Graythwaite Estate, with no public access. They were originally constructed as fishing and boating lakes for the owners of Graythwaite Hall. Great Green Hows, also known as High Tarn, is the larger of the two and lies 1km (½ mile) north of High Dam. The other, smaller pond can just be seen from the narrow road between Graythwaite and Crosslands.

HIGH DAM TARN

Grid reference: 362888   Altitude: 175m (574ft)   Depth: 10m (33ft) est.

In the village of Finsthwaite near the south-eastern shore of Windermere is the recently renovated Stott Park Bobbin Mill, once a supplier of wooden bobbins for the Lancashire cotton industry but now producing only a small number, mainly for the interest of tourists. Water supplies the power for the machinery, as it has done since the mid-nineteenth century when a small tarn north-west of the village was dammed to form High Dam Tarn.

At the start of the track leading to the tarn is a convenient car park. The tarn itself, though artificial, is undeniably beautiful and attracts many visitors. In sunny weather, rubber dinghies full of children ply back and forth and the Scots pine plantations echo to the strains of transistor radios.

The stone-faced dam at the south-eastern corner permits an outflow beneath a rustic bridge to maintain a smaller, lower dam of tree-reflecting water.

The fishing – for perch and a few brown trout – is free, apart from the statutory fishing licence.

BORETREE TARN

Grid reference: 355874	Altitude: 207m (679ft)	Depth: 12m (39ft)

This is a privately owned tarn and there is no access for the general public, but some fishing (mainly for pike and perch) is allowed for members of the Lonsdale Angling Club. Since the sixteenth century it has been part of the estate belonging to Finsthwaite House.

The tarn is approximately 1km (½ mile) south of High Dam Tarn and west of Finsthwaite. It stands on a plateau fully open to the sky, with just a few gentle tree-clad hills rising well back from its shores. The southern arm has a dense growth of white water lilies in summer.

Before being dammed in the late eighteenth century there were three small tarns here; in more recent times it has provided a domestic water supply for Finsthwaite and other nearby villages.

WHITE MOSS TARN and BLACK BECK TARN

Grid references: 334874/334871	Altitudes: 38m (125ft)/38m (125ft)
Depths: 3.5m (11½ft)/2.5m (8ft)	

Due west of Boretree Tarn and 2km (1¼ miles) across Rusland Valley is White Moss Tarn and its small companion, Black Beck Tarn. A rough track extends north from Bouth village via Burn Knott, passes between the ponds and continues beyond Low Hay Bridge as a public footpath to Rusland. Public footpaths also converge on the rough track from the road to the west, near High and Low Longmire.

The tarns are on private ground leased to the Hay Bridge Nature Reserve Society but, as both lie within a few paces of the track, they can easily be viewed.

White Moss, the larger of the two, was originally a small natural water, the outflow being dammed in 1973 to increase its surface area. At about the same time Black Beck Tarn was created from a 'boggy patch' by damming the small stream that drained it. It was planted with white water lily and great spearwort, and it's possible that it may be stocked with carp in future to control weed growth. I noticed some great reedmace (often incorrectly referred to as bulrush) in the marsh at the head of the tarn.

The larger White Moss Tarn attracts a variety of bird life so a quiet approach is recommended; a fine grey heron was motionless among the edging rush when I passed.

The nature reserve and natural history museum, to the north of the tarn, are open to members of the society and school parties by arrangement. (*About 40 minutes north from Bouth or 30 minutes south of Rusland.*)

CANNY HILL

Grid reference: 365852	Altitude: 115m (377ft)	Depth:?

Probably originally devised as a small local reservoir, this is now a private fish pond artificially embanked on three sides and guarded by a rusty barbed wire fence. Its location near a col on bare bracken-covered moorland, part of the little ridge of wild country that lies behind or east of Backbarrow, does nothing for its charm. It can be reached by footpaths from Backbarrow or from the handy car parks near Staveley-in-Cartmel used for exploring Simpson Ground Reservoir (see p. 177). The walking here is easy, pleasurable and well-signposted. (*From Chapel House, Stavely, allow 45 minutes.*)

BIGLAND TARN

Grid reference: 355829	Altitude: 158m (519ft)	Depth:?

Bigland Hall, parts of which date back a thousand years, has long been occupied by the Bigland family, the proud survivors of Norse settlement. With changing times the estate has been transformed into Bigland Hall Sporting Centre which offers riding, shooting and fishing.

Being a natural water, the tarn pre-dates the house and family. Trapped between low wooded ridges and blocked in by moraines, it is solely supplied by springs. I was told that the position of one could be seen in winter as the unfrozen area where water wells up. This could, however, simply indicate the deepest part of the tarn, the surrounding shallows freezing first. The outlet on the western side flows towards the River Leven.

Well-populated by the swans and waterfowl which nest among the sedge and rush in its north-western shallows, the tarn is used commercially as a coarse fishery. Bigland Hall is located south of the A590 and the approach, just west of Newby Bridge, is via Backbarrow and Brow Edge or Haverthwaite and Low Wood. A right of way passes through the main gates of the estate and continues past the tarn; another track from near Low Wood runs south-eastwards to join the former path beside the tarn.

Bigland Trout Fishery, an artificial lake at 364834, 1km (½ mile) north-east of Bigland Tarn, was formed by the damming of Black Beck.

Area C

East of Windermere is an undulating plateau with steep flanks falling to the lake, eastwards to the Winster Valley and south-westwards to the busy A590. This area mainly consists of poor pastureland and coniferous plantations.

GUMMERS HOW

Grid reference: 394886	Altitude: 198m (650ft)	Depth: 2m (6½ft)

Gummers How is a steep little fell. It provides a popular viewpoint near the southern end of Windermere, reached by a much-used path from the minor road that runs north-eastwards from near Newby Bridge to Strawberry Bank and Bowland Bridge. A convenient car park is set among pines on the opposite side of the road.

The fell gives its name to a reservoir, now disused, which lies at the foot of its eastern side, easily visible and closely set about by conifers. A path at the base of the fell skirts the forest but only the truly dedicated tarn-hunter would seek to penetrate the trees to reach the water margin.

A concrete dam about 1m (3ft) high, and in a poor state of repair, still holds a sizeable pond which supports a small fish population. The main plants I noted were water milfoil and broadleaved pondweed. (*From the road to Gummers How summit, allow 30–45 minutes.*)

SOW HOW

Grid reference: 401879	Altitude: 179m (587ft)	Depth:?

This is a fine artificial fish pond held by a stone-faced dam across a former streamway. A beautifully engineered spillway at the side

Sow How Tarn   A well-maintained estate fish pond complete with boathouse.

of the dam curves round to link with the original stream bed; a boathouse with weathercock completes the tranquil scene. When I visited, fish were rising, coot proclaimed their presence and sedge and water horsetail appeared to be gaining ground.

About 400m (440yds) further along the road from Gummers How car park, a narrow, metalled road on the right leads to Sow How Farm. Beyond the farmyard, a fingerpost indicates the bridleway on the left which leads past the pond. (*From Sow How Farm road end, allow 30 minutes.*) **See Walk 12.**

MIDDLE TARN (Raven's Barrow Tarn)

Grid reference: 404881	Altitude: 185m (607ft)	Depth:?

About 300m (330yds) further on from Sow How, the bridleway crosses open pastureland and enters a walled woodland through a gate. The tarn is concealed among the trees, just above eye level on

Middle Tarn Once a small reservoir, now transformed by nature into a rich water garden.

the left. A short distance from the gateway a faint path doubles back to the left and up the bank to the tarn.

This is another small, artificial reservoir or fish pond, possibly constructed in the last century. Though much overgrown with sedge and broadleaved pondweed, it is a pretty place when the rhododendrons edging the pond are in flower. Pine and alder surround it.

The path continues northwards along its edge and for a short distance through the woodland to link with another path which returns left, across a stile, towards Sow How. (*About 15 minutes from Sow How.*) See **Walk 12**.

THE HEIGHTS and DUCK TARN

Grid references: 401884/404884 Altitudes: 204m (670ft)/206m (675ft) Depths:?

Two other waters stand in the area but on private ground with no public access. The Heights is another artificial water edged by yellow iris with an islet and boathouse. To the north, massed conifers on a steep rise conceal the water from the nearby road.

Also within forbidden territory is Duck Tarn, a pond much overgrown with sedge but edged at its eastern end by white water lilies and a little bogbean. It is sunk between the steeply inclined strata of the Silurian Slates and retained by a small, leaky earth dam.

SIMPSON GROUND RESERVOIR

Grid reference: 395863   Altitude: 198m (650ft)   Depth:?

At the southern end of Windermere, Staveley-in-Cartmel stands beside a Forestry Commission plantation in the depths of which is concealed Simpson Ground Reservoir. It is a pleasant and picturesque stretch of water, providing one avoids looking at the horizontal line of the dam with its prominent railing. In winter the path skirting its northern shore is incredibly wet and muddy and a pair of wellington boots would not come amiss.

There is ample parking near the main forest road entrance at 382852. Follow the forest road to the sharp bend at its north-eastern extremity and continue along the waymarked path to the reservoir. (*Allow 45–60 minutes.*) See **Walk 12**.

FIDDLER HALL TARN

Grid reference: 391855	Altitude: 195m (640ft)	Depth: 1m (3ft)

Where the main forest road is joined by the waymarked path which enters the forest at its south-eastern boundary, this small artificial pond is just visible through the trees to the south. It lies 1km (½ mile) south-south-west of Simpson Ground Reservoir. A central island was perhaps intended to provide a safe, fox-free nesting site for water fowl. The main feature of interest when I visited was the presence of small bur-reed (*Sparganium minimum*) which I had not previously encountered. **See Walk 12.**

HELTON TARN

Grid reference: 420849	Altitude: 6m (19½ft)	Depth:?

The River Winster flows south from its source, north-east of Winster, and enters Morecambe Bay east of Grange-over-Sands. On the flat alluvial plain between the steep north–south ridges of Whitbarrow and Newton Fell, the river swells into a large pool which bears some of the characteristics of a lowland tarn. The approach is difficult, owing to the marshy surrounding ground and the fact that it is on private agricultural land, but an excellent view can be had from the back road between High Newton and Witherslack where it descends the steep eastern scarp of Newton Fell.

Although little can be discerned from this distance, the tall encircling wall of common reed with its inner ring of yellow water lilies should be visible. Helton Tarn is famous for being the grave of the first experimental iron boat, the forerunner of all modern ships, built by John Wilkinson of Lindale in the middle of the eighteenth century. He used it to transport peat from Lindale Moss to be used for smelting at Lindale ironworks in place of charcoal. How his first boat came to be submerged in Helton Tarn I have no idea, but he later built several larger iron vessels. He is buried in Lindale churchyard in an iron coffin.

Twelve
Tarn Walks

The following walks are included for those who may wish to
visit several tarns on a single excursion. Some cover what
may be fresh ground (if that is possible in Lakeland), others
are located in more popular walking areas. They vary
considerably in difficulty, from a quiet ramble around
Windermere town (Walk 1) to a hard day on the Coniston
fells (Walk 6). Sample walks are offered for each of the six
regions covered in the main text. Numbers in brackets in the
walk descriptions refer to points on the accompanying
sketch maps.

WALK 1
TARNS AROUND WINDERMERE

South-East Region, Area G   OS Map: Outdoor Leisure 7
Tarns: School Knott and Cleabarrow
Total walking time: 2½–3 hours

This short excursion, within easy walking distance of Windermere town, can be accomplished in a morning or afternoon and provides an enjoyable introduction to tarn-hunting.

First, locate Queen's Park, a large open space on the eastern side of the town. A path (1) traverses the park diagonally from Holly Road to Droomer Drive, crossing Mill Beck on the way. Follow the curve of Droomer Drive to locate the narrow lane (2) which leads out of the estate in an easterly direction and crosses Mill Beck again by a stone bridge. This footpath (2) encircles much of the eastern perimeter of the town; turn right and proceed in a southerly direction for about 400m (440yds) to the first fingerpost (3). Turn left and walk parallel to the wall to the far corner where there is a ladder stile; cross and head uphill in a south-easterly direction towards the summit of School Knott from where the tarn can be seen ahead and below.

Leave the tarn by the path which follows the outflow and at the junction with the bridleway (4) turn sharp left. Continue to the metalled lane and just past the houses look left over the low wall for the best view of Cleabarrow Tarn.

To return to Windermere, continue to the main B5284 road and turn right. Then, after 150m (165yds), turn right again by Cleabarrow House to follow the Dales Way, indicated by a fingerpost, over fields to a minor road by Matson Ground Estate Farm. Continue along the path on the other side of the road and beside the farm; beyond the first gate take the right-hand path (5), leading north-west towards the beautiful Helm Farm. Continue in a northerly direction, skirting the bungalows, to where two fingerposts are confusingly placed almost side by side (6). Whichever you decide to follow, walking in a northerly direction will take you to Park Road. Keep advancing north for 500m (550yds) to reach your original starting point at Queen's Park.

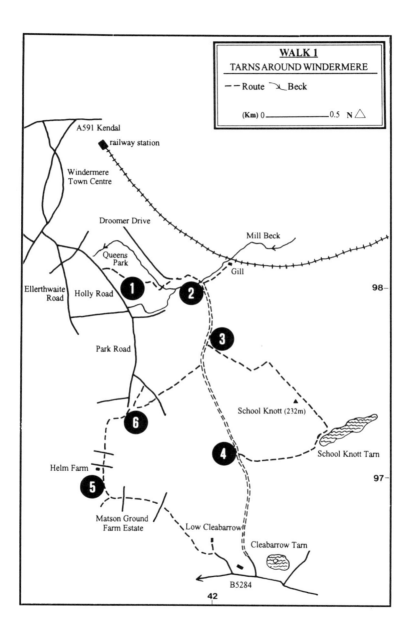

WALK 2
TARNS AROUND GRASMERE

South-East Region, Area A   OS Map: Outdoor Leisure 7
Tarns: White Moss, Alcock and Dockey
Total walking time: 2–3 hours

If starting from the Grasmere car parks (P), walk to Dove Cottage and the Wordsworth Museum just across the A591. Continue up the road, past the fingerpost to Alcock Tarn and the duck pond on the left. At the seat and second fingerpost (1) indicating Alcock Tarn, continue along the metalled road for about 3 minutes to White Moss Tarn (2).

If starting from the Rydal Water quarry car parks, the rough track from the eastern end climbs above the quarry to White Moss Tarn (2). Here you may wish to spend a short while exploring White Moss Common. Then return to the seat and fingerpost (1) and take the unsurfaced track to Alcock Tarn. After a few paces, you are faced with a choice between the gentler, winding path through the gate and past a small artificial pond, or the steeper track right. Both routes lead to the tarn.

There is no distinct path to Dockey Tarn (3). Sheep trods may be followed, though this is difficult in summer when the bracken is dense. Be careful not to lose altitude for Dockey is some 12m (39ft) above Alcock, which is why the latter can just be seen from Dockey, but not the reverse.

It is possible to return to the Coffin Road and White Moss Tarn from here by descending north-westwards and westwards across the head of Dunney Beck to pick up a very steep path, badly eroded in parts, which descends the valley of the beck. But to complete the round to Grasmere, return to Alcock Tarn and continue northwards on the distinct path which descends into the valley of Greenhead Gill, passing the Thirlmere–Manchester water conduit and the seat dedicated to Tennyson (Tim) Oldfield, to arrive at the gate (4), which gives access to a metalled lane. At the end, turn left and continue down the road to the Swan Hotel.

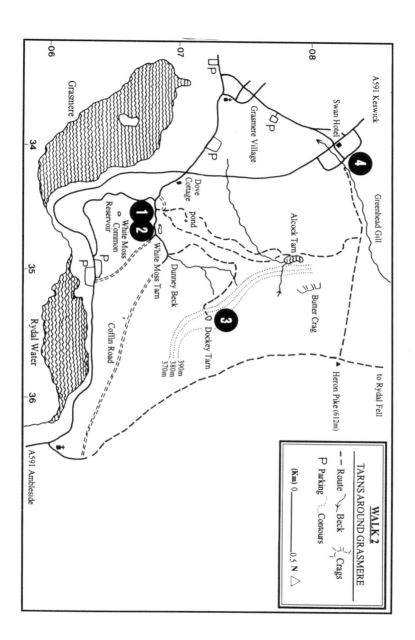

WALK 2
TARNS AROUND GRASMERE

- - - Route ⌇ Beck ⅄⅄ Crags
P Parking ⋮ Contours

(Km) 0 _____ 0.5 N △

A591 Keswick

Greenhead Gill

Swan Hotel

Grasmere Village

P

P

Grasmere

Dove Cottage

pond

Alcock Tarn

Butter Crag

Heron Pike (612m)

to Rydal Fell

White Moss Common
Reservoir

White Moss Tarn

Dunney Beck

Dockey Tarn

390m
380m
370m

Coffin Road

Rydal Water

A591 Ambleside

WALK 3
CLAIFE HEIGHTS TARNS

South-East Region, Area E   OS Map: Outdoor Leisure 7
Tarns: Brownstone, High Moss, Scale Head, Wise Een and Moss Eccles
Total walking time: 4–5 hours

I have always found Claife Heights a particularly appealing ridge; its undulating form and mixture of forest, moor and pasture mean that one can never see far ahead and there is always something of interest over the next rise. Its modest elevation of up to 270m (886ft) at High Blind How makes this an ideal area for getting into walking trim; it is also a superb viewpoint, with vistas across Windermere to the east and broad panoramas westwards towards the Coniston Fells and the Langdales.

Parking is available at the bottom of the hill beyond Far Sawrey, near the ferry terminal; there is also a very small car park by the telephone kiosk at Near Sawrey. At the northern end is Red Nab car park, accessible along a single-track road from High Wray. This walk starts from the car park near the ferry landing but could be adjusted if you prefer to start from one of the others.

From the rear end of the car park, climb the steep path to the station ruin (1). Pass through the main arch and between the cleft rocks on the left, to follow the zigzag path, occasionally marked with white-topped posts, up the steep hillside. This is the worst climb of the day! After the exertion you may wish to stop and enjoy the views across the lake. . . From here, follow the signs to Hawkshead. Go through a gate on to a walled lane (2) and proceed left along it to the first right-hand turning (3). The path climbs, then levels out, before curving around another small pond, at 382962, and entering the woodland. Continue northwards along the undulating path, taking the uphill fork, until a clear viewpoint on the right offers views over Thompson's Holm Island (4). Return to the track and take the left-hand path (5) which is signed to Hawkshead. This takes you into the forest, passing over some interesting rock outcrops on the way. Cross a forest road and foot-bridge (6) to arrive at the viewpoint and trig. station at High Blind How (7).

After a pause to enjoy the view, continue to the broad forest track (8), turn left, and then right at the junction with the forest

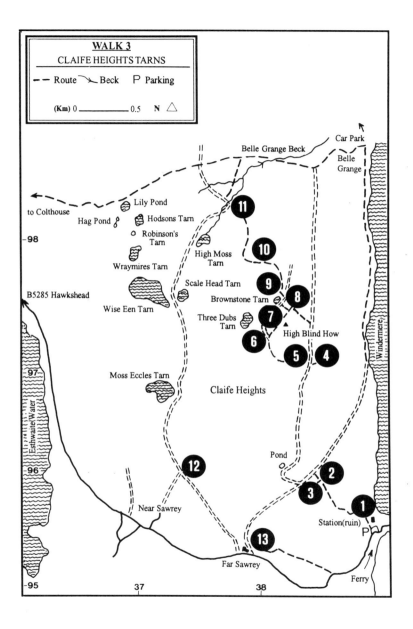

WALK 3

CLAIFE HEIGHTS TARNS

‒ ‒ Route ⟋ Beck P Parking

(Km) 0 _____ 0.5 N △

Car Park

Belle Grange Beck

Belle Grange

Lily Pond

to Colthouse

Hag Pond

Hodsons Tarn

Robinson's Tarn

Wraymires Tarn

High Moss Tarn

‒98

Scale Head Tarn

B5285 Hawkshead

Wise Een Tarn

Brownstone Tarn

Three Dubs Tarn

High Blind How

‒97

Moss Eccles Tarn

Claife Heights

Esthwaite Water

‒96

Pond

Near Sawrey

Station(ruin) P

Far Sawrey

‒95

Ferry

37   38

Windermere

road. Nearby is Brownstone Tarn, a small, silted, artificial pond. Take the left-hand path (9) into the forest again, ascending eventually to another rocky viewpoint (10), where deer can sometimes be seen. Then descend to reach a forest road at a sharp bend (11). A left turn here will bring you to High Moss Tarn after 400m (440yds). Continue along this bridle track in a generally southerly direction, to pass the remaining tarns: Scale Head, Wise Een and Moss Eccles in turn. Beyond Moss Eccles, take the appropriate signposted path at the fork (12) to Far Sawrey. Just past the Sawrey Hotel, a fingerpost (13) indicates a short cut back to the road near the car park.

WALK 4
FOUR TARNS LOW LEVEL WALK

South-East Region, Area C   OS Map: Outdoor Leisure 7
Tarns: Tarn Hows (The Tarns), High Arnside Tarn, Holme Ground Tarns and Yew Tree Tarn
Total walking time: 3–3½ hours

On a day when the tops are misted, this is an ideal low-level walk, rising to a maximum altitude of just over 280m (920ft); it's even more relaxing and enjoyable in sunshine. By consulting the Ordnance Survey map, the walk can easily be extended or shortened to suit your requirements.

The most convenient starting point is the National Trust Tom Gill car park, at 322999, on the A593 Coniston to Skelwith Bridge road, 3km (2 miles) north of Coniston.

From the car park (1), cross the bridge over Tom Gill and walk up the main path in an easterly direction, keeping an eye open for the path sign beside the gill, just before the falls. Follow the gill upstream to the dam (2) which retains Tarn Hows.

If you have plenty of time, it's well worth walking right round the tarn in order to appreciate its splendours fully. There are many minor paths, but the occasionally signed 'main path' on either side of the tarn will lead you to a crossing (3). Here you should take the northerly, level path, to arrive at a walled lane (4). High Arnside Tarn can just be seen ahead, across the field. Follow the lane left until you are abreast of this tarn, which is through a rusty iron gate on the right. Continue northwards along the lane and in 15

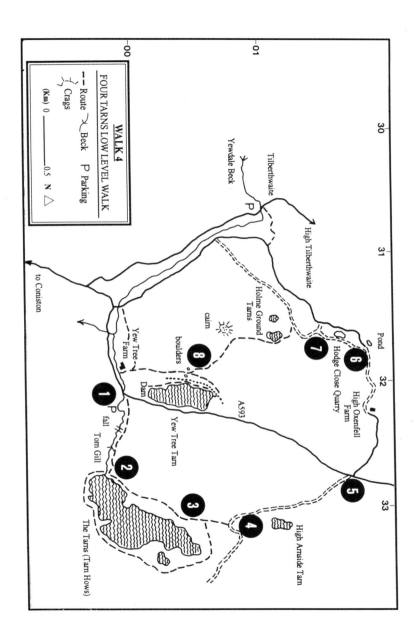

WALK 4
FOUR TARNS LOW LEVEL WALK

- - Route   ⅄ Beck   P Parking
⅄ Crags
(Km) 0 ————— 0.5   N △

00
01

30
31
32
33

Yewdale Beck
Tilberthwaite
P
High Tilberthwaite

to Coniston

Holme Ground Tarns
cairn
boulders
Yew Tree Farm
Dam
8
7
Pond
Hodge Close Quarry
6
High Oxenfell Farm

Yew Tree Tarn
A593

1
fall
Tom Gill
2
3
High Arnside Tarn
4
5

The Tarns (Tarn Hows)

minutes you will arrive at High Cross, beside Arnside Cottage (5).

Cross the A593 and head along the metalled lane to High Oxenfell Farm. Continue through the gate to the stony track beyond, passing through another gate 300m (330yds) further on, at the farm boundary. Now keep an eye open for an overgrown pond on the right (busy with dragonflies and damsel flies when I passed). Opposite is a gate (6) which gives access to a broad, grassy bridleway leading directly towards Holme Ground Tarns. Alternatively, you may choose to continue on the track, past the pond and between cottages, to Hodge Close Quarry where outdoor pursuits enthusiasts practise abseiling on the sheer rock walls and aqualung diving in the deep green waters at the bottom.

The bridleway leading to Holme Ground Tarns may be regained through a gateway (7) at the southern end of the quarry.

Continue southwards along the bridleway and just beyond a gate take the sharp left-hand track past piles of quarry waste. Then follow either of the two uphill paths to Holme Ground Tarns. The smaller companion to the main tarn can be sought some 50m (55yds) to the west, though it cannot compare scenically with its larger neighbour.

Beyond the main tarn a cairned height can be seen; the path round the east side leads directly towards it, but soon slips to the left over a grassy shoulder at 280m (920ft). The path then descends steadily into a stony gully, occasionally cairned, and eases beneath oak and birch. Suddenly the northern end of Yew Tree Tarn, the next objective, is seen ahead. A short distance beyond, the path arrives at a junction (8) where there is a waymark between two large boulders.

Turn left along the level track which shortly curves right to pass through the stone wall encircling the tarn. From the giant spaced pines that grow at the head of this artificial water, follow the initially indistinct path southwards along the west side of the water to the dam at the far end. Cross the dam and walk south down the road for about 5 minutes to get back to Tom Gill car park (1).

An alternative starting point is the car park at Low Tilberthwaite, 307010, beside Yewdale Beck. From here, cross the bridge, then the padlocked wooden beam, to follow the left-hand side of the beck eastwards. Walk across the slaty ground towards the gate into the woodland known as Low Coppice, then follow the path to the track and walk right to reach the metalled road. Follow the road left, or north-eastwards, for 500m (550yds), past Holme Ground Farm, to Hodge Close Quarry. Here you are at the gateway (7) at the southern end of the quarry. This gives access to the bridleway and thence to Holme Ground Tarns, adding about half an hour to a 3-hour walk.

WALK 5
LANGDALE PIKES

South-West Region, Area E   OS Map: Outdoor Leisure 6
Tarns: Stickle Tarn
Total walking time: 3–4 hours

Langdale is one of the most popular areas in Lakeland for walkers and climbers. The resulting over-use, allied to the general steepness of all the popular fell routes here, has led to the severe erosion of footpaths, turning them into unsightly and sometimes dangerous chutes of rock and rubble. If the income from the parking charges imposed here by the National Trust is used to tackle the footpath problem it will certainly be money well spent.

There are three convenient car parks at the head of Langdale, two near the New Dungeon Ghyll Hotel and one beside the Old Dungeon Ghyll Hotel.

If starting from either of the New Dungeon Ghyll Hotel car parks, aim for the high ground; there is a gate at the head of Stickle Ghyll Park which gives access to the Stickle Ghyll track. From the car park south of the valley road, walk past the hotel and through the gate to join the above track.

After 100m (110yds), take the left-hand branch and head towards a gateway which is clearly visible on the near skyline. At the gate (2), where the path from the Old Dungeon Ghyll car park joins the track, head right (or left if coming from the Old Dungeon Ghyll) uphill. Where the path touches the watercourse of the Dungeon Ghyll, cross on stepping stones (3) so that the ghyll is on your right. (Another equally valid path (3a), partially improved but not so convenient for this round, may be gained by continuing a further 150m (165yds) uphill before turning left. It runs parallel to our chosen path but on the opposite side of the ghyll.)

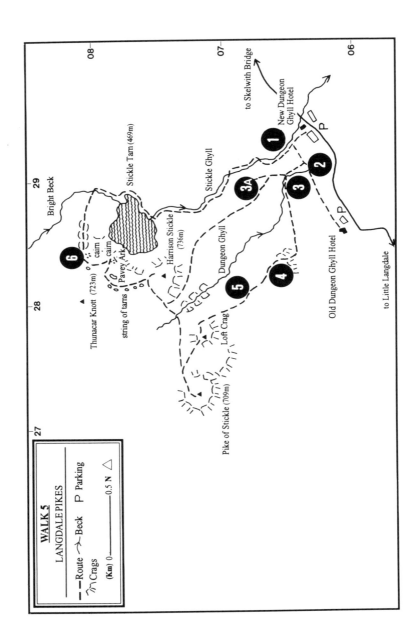

WALK 5
LANGDALE PIKES

- - - Route   →- Beck   P Parking
⌒⌒ Crags
(Km) 0 ————— 0.5 N △

to Skelwith Bridge

New Dungeon
Ghyll Hotel
P

to Little Langdale

Old Dungeon Ghyll Hotel
P

Stickle Ghyll

Dungeon Ghyll

Stickle Tarn (469m)

Bright Beck

Harrison Stickle
(736m)

Pavey Ark
cairn
cairn
string of tarns

Thunacar Knott (723m)

Loft Crag

Pike of Stickle (709m)

06
07
08

27
28
29

After crossing the ghyll, continue up the steep, eroded path to the thyme-covered rocks, bearing right up a short rock gully to a terrace, then left through a rock gateway (4) to easier, grassy ground. From here may be seen the grey flanks of Thorn Crag and Harrison Stickle, with the ravine of Dungeon Ghyll between.

Continue left towards the grim wall of Gimmer Crag and the brown scar of the eroded path for the final scramble. At the top, the hump of Loft Crag is on the left, bearing a strong resemblance to the still concealed Pike o' Stickle, a misconception which is soon resolved as you scale Loft Crag.

Approaching the Pike, you pass the head of a scree gully. Here a notice warns that the Neolithic 'axe factory' site below is being progressively obliterated by thousands of tons of scree and urges voluntary restraint by potential scree runners. The ascent of the Pike itself cannot be achieved without tackling a mild 'bad step'; there is a choice of two on clean rock on the north-western side. Above is the summit cairn at 709m (2,325ft).

After descending by the same route, proceed eastwards across the easier ground of Harrison Combe to Harrison Stickle, where there are no difficulties in reaching the cairn at 736m (2,414ft).

North of the summit, and between it and the cliffs of Pavey Ark, is a wide gully and steep path which permits descent to Stickle Tarn if required.

Cross the head of the gully and follow the not-too-distinct paths which circle behind Pavey Ark itself. Between it and Thunacar Knott are several unnamed tarns, some containing bogbean, others trimmed with cotton grass. A pleasant hour may be spent exploring or lounging beside these pretty ponds.

Return to the cliffs and summit cairn of Pavey Ark and follow the edge north-eastwards to another prominent cairn which stands at the head of an eastward-sloping gully (6). This was described as 'grassy' by Wainwright but has long since been stripped of its turf; it is shown as a path on the Ordnance Survey map. Descend with care to Bright Beck and walk downstream to Stickle Tarn.

From the dam, take the downhill path beside the outflow towards the New Dungeon Ghyll Hotel and the start of the walk. Beware the reconstructed section of the path with its downward-sloping stones – fine for climbing up but lethal when descending in wet conditions.

WALK 6
THE CONISTON ROUND

South-West Region, Area G   OS Map: Outdoor Leisure 6
Tarns: Boo Tarn, Blind Tarn, Goat's Water, Low Water and Levers Water
Total walking time: 5–6 hours

This is a slight variation on a very popular walk, involving a south–north traverse of the main ridge of the Coniston Massif, visiting – or viewing – the five named tarns that lie to the east of it. The longer approach via the Walna Scar Road, avoiding the steep, quarry-flanked tourist route up the Old Man, is in my opinion much to be preferred. It also enables the walker to enjoy the full length of this fine ridge, while leaving escape routes if time or weather conditions dictate.

A convenient starting point is the car park at the head of the narrow, metalled road which rises steeply from the centre of Coniston, opposite Lake Road. This road takes you past the old railway station and the car park lies just beyond the fell gate.

From the car park (1), walk westwards along the Walna Scar Road. Where the quarry track branches right up the hill, Boo Tarn will be found 10m (11yds) beyond, on the opposite side. About 1km (½ mile) further along, a broad, grassy track on the right leads to Goat's Water. Continue along the Walna Scar road to where a bridge (2) crosses the outflow from that tarn. From the north-western balustrade, you can see ahead the sweep of high ground, behind which you will be climbing. Note, from left to right, the piles of quarry waste, the pocket containing Blind Tarn, and the dark precipice of Dow Crag.

Beyond the bridge the track rises steadily. Some two-thirds of the way up the scar, look out for an isolated cairn (3) which marks the structured path on the right leading to a disused quarry. Where the path rises and curves left, leave it for the hummocky ground and maintain the same contour leftwards until you reach the tarn.

Rejoin the Walna Scar Road and continue to the top of the scarp, where you turn right and follow the worn path to the summit of Brown Pike. Continue in a northerly direction, past Buck Pike to Dow Crag, with views of Goat's Water below. On the descent to Goat's Hawse (4), the summit of the Old Man and the stony path to it can be seen as it curves right and upwards to the

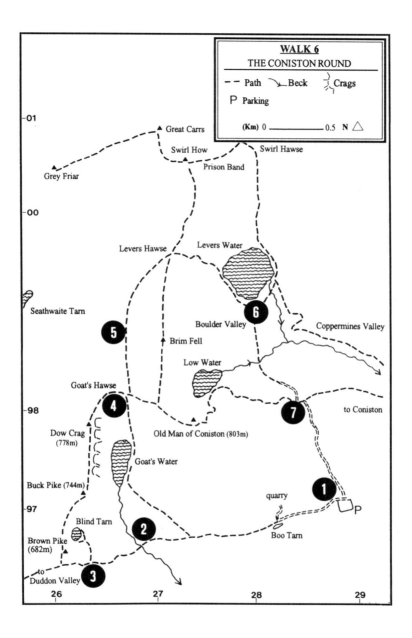

-01

▲ Great Carrs

Swirl How ▲

Swirl Hawse

Prison Band

▲ Grey Friar

-00

Levers Hawse

Levers Water

Seathwaite Tarn

5

6

Boulder Valley

Coppermines Valley

▲ Brim Fell

Low Water

Goat's Hawse

4

-98

7

to Coniston

Dow Crag
(778m)

Old Man of Coniston (803m)

Goat's Water

Buck Pike (744m)

quarry

1

-97

Blind Tarn

2

P

Brown Pike
(682m)

Boo Tarn

to
Duddon Valley

3

26   27   28   29

cairn. Here you can follow the colourful crowds to pay homage to Coniston's premier fell. (The tourist path from the top descends by way of Low Water to lower altitudes if need be. The walk can then be completed by turning right at the junction (7) to take the path back to the car park.)

From the summit of the Old Man, skirt the edge that overlooks Low Water, proceed northwards over gentle Brim Fell and descend to Levers Hawse, with views to Levers Water. The steep, unstable gully which descends to Levers Water is the final escape route, but this exit is not recommended.

(At this point it's worth mentioning a way of avoiding the Old Man, should crowds or time press. An excellent but little-used path (5) sneaks behind the Old Man's back along the fell's western flank. It can be clearly seen from a distance when descending Dow Crag to Goat's Hawse, but its start is difficult to find close to. The path begins a short distance up from Goat's Hawse, from a green marshy patch; look out for a small white cairn 20m (22yds) away, on the left of the summit path. The path leads easily and directly to Levers Hawse.)

From Levers Hawse, continue along the ridge to climb to Swirl How in 30–40 minutes, noting part of Seathwaite Tarn away to the left. This is a fine top, with magnificent views of mountain scenery all about, and a full-length vista of the ridge that has just been traversed.

The descent to Levers Water is by way of the ridge known as Prison Band which descends eastwards from the summit. From the col at the bottom – Swirl Hawse – take the path on the right to Levers Water.

The final leg of the walk, a gentle downhill stroll, begins from the southern corner of the tarn via a col (6) between the fenced-off mine shafts and the rising ground to their right. This leads to the aptly named Boulder Valley where the downhill path crosses the outflow from Low Water, which descends some 150m (490ft) by a series of cascades and falls, from the tarn.

Continue to the disused quarry from where a fine track leads to the main tourist route up to the Old Man. Turn left at the junction (7), then bear right, keeping to the slaty track which takes you back to the Walna Scar Road car park (1).

WALK 7
HAYESWATER AND ANGLE TARN

North-East Region, Area B   OS Map: Outdoor Leisure 5
Tarns: Hayeswater and Angle Tarn
Total walking time: 3 hours

This is a short walk for those wishing to find their fell legs. It begins at Hartsop village, near Brothers Water (now regarded as a minor lake, though it was considered a tarn in the early nineteenth century).

Park at Cow Bridge, 403134, or at the head of the village where there is limited parking at 410131.

From the A592, head through the village, past the sheep pens and along the metalled track leading to the filter house. Look out for the right-hand fork (1) which leads to the bridge over Hayeswater Gill and climbs on the true left side of the gill to the tarn. It is also possible to continue on the former track to the filter house, to pass it on the right, and to descend to the gill. This may be crossed by a narrow foot-bridge, after which you follow a steep path to join the track to the Hayeswater dam (2).

Cross the outflow by means of the foot-bridge and head up the hillside to the junction with the Angle Tarn–High Street path (3). Turn left to follow this path over peat bog and between the crags until Angle Tarn's convoluted shoreline hoves into view.

The way then circles the north shore of the tarn which is soon hidden from sight as you swing right. Here you can enjoy the delights of the narrow path that clings to the hillside and affords glorious views left towards the Helvellyn range and its coves and behind towards Brothers Water and the Kirkstone Pass.

After negotiating the sharp bend (4) around the head of Dubhow Beck, where the path is supported by wooden shuttering, the way descends past two cairns. Beyond, there are views of Ullswater as you descend to Boredale Hause where a small, level, grassy area is separated from a ruined sheepfold by Stonebarrow Gill (5). Take the left-hand fork, crossing the gill to head in a southerly direction back towards Brothers Water. At the bottom, where the path skirts Goldrill Beck, continue on the same line to the prominent Angletarn Beck and its falls (6). If returning to Cow Bridge, cross the foot-bridge and go through the gate on the right

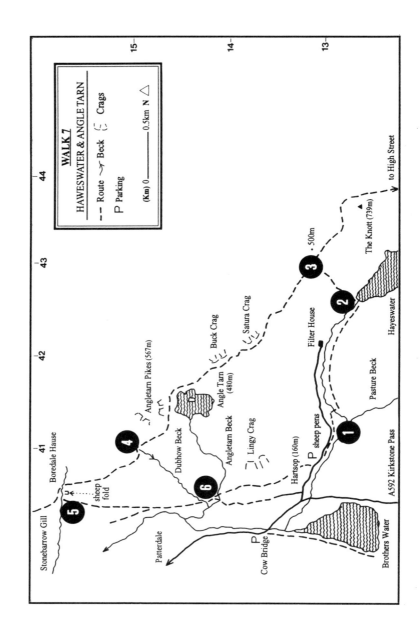

WALK 7
HAWESWATER & ANGLE TARN

- - - Route ⌇ Beck ⌇⌇ Crags

P Parking

(Km) 0 ——————— 0.5km N △

The Knott (739m)

to High Street

· 500m

Hayeswater

Filter House

Satura Crag

Buck Crag

Angletarn Pikes (567m)

Angle Tarn (480m)

Pasture Beck

A592 Kirkstone Pass

Hartsop (160m)

P sheep pens

Angletarn Beck

Lingy Crag

Dubhow Beck

Boredale Hause

Stonebarrow Gill

sheep fold

Patterdale

P Cow Bridge

Brothers Water

for the last leg to the lower end of the village. If making for Upper Hartsop, take the ladder stile left and uphill for the path to the village car park.

WALK 8
TWO WATERS WALK

North-East Region, Area C   OS Map: Outdoor Leisure 5
Tarns: Blea Water and Small Water
Total walking time: 3–4 hours

The head of Haweswater (Mardale Head) is a popular parking spot for both walkers and sightseers. Nevertheless, with ingenuity and determination one can usually find a place nearby.

This is the starting point for many different expeditions over these fascinating eastern fells. This area offers high-level walking at its best, but it can also severely test one's route-finding abilities, particularly in conditions of poor visibility. The circuit described is specifically designed to view the two tarns, but could easily be extended or modified according to your requirements. The steep craggy ascent of the Riggindale Ridge offers an interesting 'mountaineering' approach to High Street, not suitable for the nervous, or for school parties. It involves an ascent of some 560m (1,837ft).

From just beyond the car park, take the 'Bampton' footpath which crosses Mardale Beck (1), the main inflow into Haweswater. Head to the right along the shore, towards The Rigg; here the path skirts a conifer plantation. Just before reaching the gap in the wall (2), double back on the steeply rising, grassy path through the bracken leading to the rocky arête. After a series of scrambles over minor crags (Swine, Heron and Eagle), the slope eases and the increasing altitude offers expanding views into Riggindale on the northern side of the ridge and to Blea Water which comes into view slightly to your left. Further left, Small Water can also be seen. The clearly defined path follows the crest of the ridge all the way. After Rough Crag, the highest point on the ridge and almost directly above Blea Water, the path descends to the col of Caspel Gate (3), where a couple of ephemeral tarns are situated.

(At this point, an alternative approach from Mardale Beck joins the ridge. After crossing the beck (1), turn left and traverse the

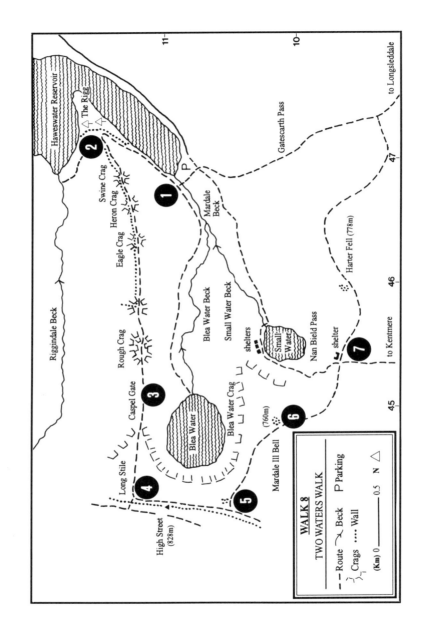

WALK 8
TWO WATERS WALK

Route — Beck P Parking
Crags .... Wall
(Km) 0 —— 0.5 N △

often wet slopes to the impressive corrie which retains Blea Water. From its outflow, proceed north-westwards along a faint track up grassy moraine to gain the col at Caspel Gate.)

From here the ridge steepens for the final approach to the shoulder of High Street. The rocky scrambles are not particularly difficult but care should still be taken. On reaching the wall (4) at the top, turn left and follow the path in a southerly direction, past the concrete trig. point to a cairn. This is where the wall-hugging path is abandoned in favour of a sharp left turn (5). Follow the new path to the summit of Mardale Ill Bell (6), safely skirting the dangerous Blea Water Crag which falls to the now unseen tarn. Continue in a general south-easterly direction, gradually descending to the summit of Nan Bield Pass (7). Here a wall-like cairn or shelter marks the beginning of an eroded but not too difficult descent leftwards to Small Water.

Where the path skirts the tarn, there are three small rock shelters which once offered refuge to travellers caught in winter storms. Continue along the path beside the tarn to cross the outflow and descend to the car park at the head of Haweswater.

WALK 9
A RAMBLE AROUND LOWESWATER

North-West Region, Area B   OS Map: Outdoor Leisure 4
Tarns: High Nook Tarn
Total walking time: 2½–3 hours

This pleasant ramble through National Trust property makes an ideal walk for those seeking an easy day away from the high fells. It covers about 8km (5 miles) and just 200m (656ft) of ascent. There are three handy car parks, two at the north-western end of Loweswater on the Loweswater to Mockerkin road, 122223 and 118224, and one at the south-eastern end by Maggie's Bridge, 134210, where there is room for up to eight considerately parked cars. The two former car parks at Waterend are larger and I prefer to start there.

The path begins from a roadside stile beside a telephone kiosk (1) and follows a hedgerow for 50m (55yds). At the next stile, turn right to cross a meadow and a froggy marsh by duckboards, then join the metalled lane to Hudson Place. Bear left to take the

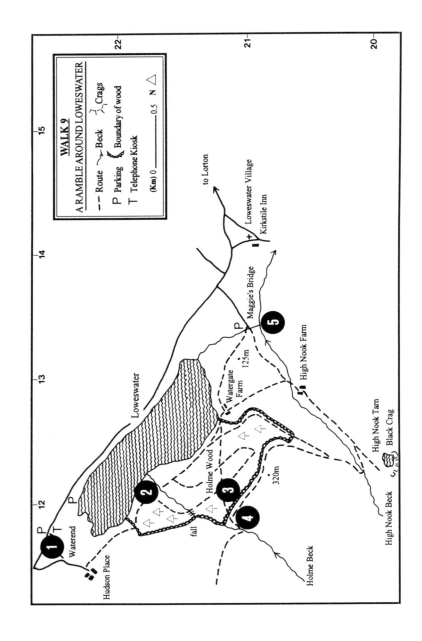

WALK 9
A RAMBLE AROUND LOWESWATER

— — Route ～ Beck
P Parking ⟨ Boundary of wood
T Telephone Kiosk

(Km) 0 ————— 0.5   N △

Loweswater

to Lorton

Loweswater Village

Kirkstile Inn

Maggie's Bridge

P

Waterend

Hudson Place

fall

Holme Wood

Watergate Farm

125m

320m

High Nook Farm

High Nook Tarm

Black Crag

High Nook Beck

Holme Beck

signed, gated track towards Loweswater shore. Running parallel with the lake shore, this track enters pleasant woodland through another gate.

Take the first forest track to the right (2) and walk uphill to where Holme Force descends in a series of short falls and cascades, spectacular in spate. The final twin falls of some 6m (19½ft) descend on either side of a tree-surmounted, green-draped crag. On a bright spring morning the leaf-filtered light will delight the eye of the photographer. However the upper fall is dangerous and an approach should not be attempted.

Continue along the forest track for some 400m (440yds) to where a prominent path crosses at an angle (3). Turn right up the path, taking care to avoid the many black dungbeetles hurrying uphill, until you reach the boundary wall of Holme Wood. Cross the ladder stile and join the level path on the open fellside (4). Follow this path left, or south-eastwards, as it skirts the woodland wall and bends right to descend to the valley of Highnook Beck. Cross the beck and head due south for High Nook Tarn which lies beneath Black Crag.

To return, follow the grassy track downhill and north-eastwards, parallel with the beck, through High Nook Farm to Maggie's Bridge (5). If refreshment is required at this point, I would recommend a 10-minute deviation to the Kirkstile Inn, 500m (550yds) along the road to the south-east.

From Maggie's Bridge, take the level, gated track towards the lake and Watergate Farm, bearing right here to follow the lake shore. Cross Holme Beck and retrace the outward trek to Hudson Place and the car park.

WALK 10
TO DALE HEAD AND DALEHEAD TARN

North-West Region, Area D   OS Map: Outdoor Leisure 4
Tarns: Dalehead, Launchy and High Scawdel
Total walking time: 4–4½ hours

The starting point is a small car park at 232194, beside Chapel Bridge, just south-west of Little Town. Walk back 100m (110yds) up the hill towards Little Town and cross the stile on the right (1). Follow the track right for 1km (½ mile) until you are opposite the

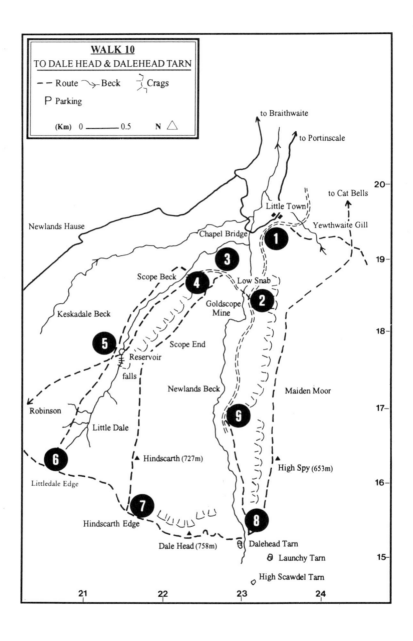

WALK 10
TO DALE HEAD & DALEHEAD TARN

- - Route   ⌐⌐Beck   Crags

P Parking

(Km) 0 ———— 0.5   N △

to Braithwaite

to Portinscale

to Cat Bells

20—

Little Town

Yewthwaite Gill

Newlands Hause

Chapel Bridge

19—

3

Scope Beck

4   Low Snab

Goldscope Mine

2

Keskadale Beck

18—

5   Scope End

Reservoir

falls

Newlands Beck

Maiden Moor

Robinson

17—

9

Little Dale

▲ Hindscarth (727m)

6

High Spy (653m)

16—

Littledale Edge

7

Hindscarth Edge

8

▲ Dale Head (758m)   Dalehead Tarn

ᴓ Launchy Tarn

15—

◌ High Scawdel Tarn

21   22   23   24

Goldscope Mine spoil heaps (2). Curve right with the stone wall and cross the beck by the foot-bridge to gain the track at Low Snab. Leaving the spoil heaps on your left, head up the slope, with Causey's hump ahead, to reach the track that rounds the nose of the ridge (3). Macho types may wish to take the path straight up the nose on to the ridge and head south-west and south for Hindscarth, a fine ridge walk with an interesting scramble on the way. We will meet up with them later on Hindscarth Edge (7).

Those looking for gentler pleasures should keep to the track, curving leftwards around the nose and into the valley of Scope Beck. At the mine workings the track dips towards the beck: do not follow. Instead, scramble over the workings and locate a new track a few paces higher up (4). This soon narrows to a thin but clear and level path. Eventually a window or gap will appear in the rock wall that encloses the head of the valley. Also ahead, at path height, is a level grassy bank across the valley with a short stairway of white water at its far left-hand corner if there has been recent rain.

This is the dam and spillway of a small reservoir (5), perhaps once associated with mining operations. Trout, I am told, have been seen here. Littledale Falls, which are impressive in wet conditions, can be seen descending in the gorge ahead.

Cross the valley and beck and climb up to a substantial grassy track, bouldery in places, which rises over the shoulder to the right of the falls. Entering the secret hanging valley of Little Dale, the path thins and swings right to avoid bog, skirts beneath screes and outcrops and then fades away. A higher path may be followed further but in the end it is just a matter of slogging it out for the last few hundred metres to gain Littledale Edge (6), with its fence. From here one may look across to Honister Crag and to the pass far below.

Turn left, or south-eastwards, along the switchback ridge to meet the path from Hindscarth which comes in from the left (7). Continue along Hindscarth Edge to Dale Head (identified by its tall, slim cairn) and begin to descend eastwards.

Ahead and slightly to your right you will see the two peat moss ponds of Launchy Tarn and High Scawdel Tarn on the green plateau; then, below, Dalehead Tarn itself. To the left, two alternative return routes can be viewed and assessed. Macho types will take the high road over High Spy and Maiden Moor to the col before Cat Bells, then descend westwards on the left side of Yewthwaite Gill towards Little Town. The low road descends into the valley of Newlands Beck; the path can be seen as a lighter line slanting across the screes far below High Spy.

Now descend the steep, eroded path to Dalehead Tarn and, if time permits, climb up to the peat moss tarns.

The water that drains from Dalehead Tarn and becomes Newlands Beck descends to the valley through a shallow ravine. Avoid this by taking the broad path towards High Spy but after a few paces branch left and downhill at a small cairn (8), to join the right bank of the beck once it has cleared the ravine. Here you can pick up a cairned path but you will need to follow it carefully as it rambles between boulders to the flatter green of the lower hanging valley. Keep well to the right of the beck and falls to join the scree path which can be seen ahead. Once this path is gained, there are no further problems. It descends to join the valley track and eventually the outward trail opposite the Goldscope Mine spoil heaps (2).

WALK 11
TO LITTLE TARN, ORTHWAITE

Outlying Tarns North, Area A	**OS Map: Landranger 90**

Tarns: Overwater and Little Tarn
Total walking time: 3 hours

This low-level walk on unfrequented but waymarked paths provides a pleasant day off from the high fells. As it traverses stock-filled pasture land, it is advisable to leave the dog at home.

Begin from the eastern side of Bassenthwaite village green where a fingerpost beside an orchard wall indicates 'Public Bridleway, Peter House Farm'. Follow the narrow lane to its end where a stile beside the gate gives access to a meadow. Follow the hedgerow left to the next stile and continue on the same line to the next. Beyond, the path (1) angles right for Peter House Farm but our route continues straight ahead, via another path, to skirt High Close. In the corner of the field beyond the house, pass through the gateway left (2) and cross two fields to a gate facing right, at the end of the fence. Pass through and circle down the steep bank to

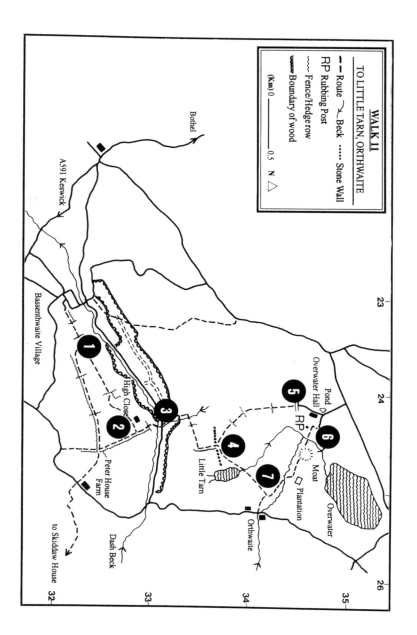

WALK 11
TO LITTLE TARN, ORTHWAITE

- – – Route
- RP Rubbing Post
- ∿ Fence/Hedgerow
- ⌁ Boundary of wood
- ＞ Beck
- ⋯⋯ Stone Wall

(Km) 0 ——— 0.5   N △

Bothel

A591 Keswick

Bassenthwaite Village

High Close

Peter House Farm

Dash Beck

to Skiddaw House

Little Tarn

Overwater Hall

Pond

RP

Moat

Plantation

Overwater

Orthwaite

1 2 3 4 5 6 7

23 24 26

32 33 34 35

Dash Beck, cross by the foot-bridge and turn right to reach the road (3). Opposite, take the signed path through the trees which clothe the steep scarp, noting the interesting vertical strata of the Skiddaw Slates in the stream bed.

At the top, cross the stile right, then the beck, and follow the broad track to catch the first glimpse of Little Tarn below in the valley. Where the broad track continues through the gate and down the hill, do not follow. Instead go left along the hedgerow to the clearly visible ladder stile and fingerpost (4). Cross the wall by the stile and follow the Overwater direction. At the second stile beyond the fingerpost, angle right, or northwards, and downhill along the course of an old bridleway to a gateway, then through a double-gated pen to a lane (5). You will pass Overwater Hall on the right, then a duck pond on the left. Here, turn right, along a lane. When you see a gate and sign on the right, go through into the meadow where the bust of a top-hatted Regency buck stands atop a rectangular stone rubbing post. (Who was he, this proud fellow, doomed to eternal indignity?)

With Overwater Hall at your back, head for the double gates and the bridge (6) which crosses the tranquil stream that flows to Overwater. Pass the moat and head towards the fenced, dark conifer plantation. Beside it, angle right to cross the beck by a foot-bridge, then left to the gate and stile. At the end of the hedgerow you will be near the road at Orthwaite (7). Circle right to go through the gate and stile; then follow the fence left and downhill towards Little Tarn, to cross its outflow by the bridge. Brave the rushes to your left and slant uphill beneath the trees, through the gorse and above the tarn, curving right until you reach the fingerpost (4).

Retrace your earlier steps to the road (3), then turn right to walk about 1.5km (1 mile) back to Bassenthwaite village.

WALK 12
FOREST WALKS AT STAVELEY-IN-CARTMEL

Outlying Tarns South, Area C   OS Map: Landranger 96
Tarns: Fiddler Hall, Sow How, Middle and Simpson Ground Reservoir
Total walking time: 3–4 hours

Parking is available at the forest road entrance, in a layby opposite

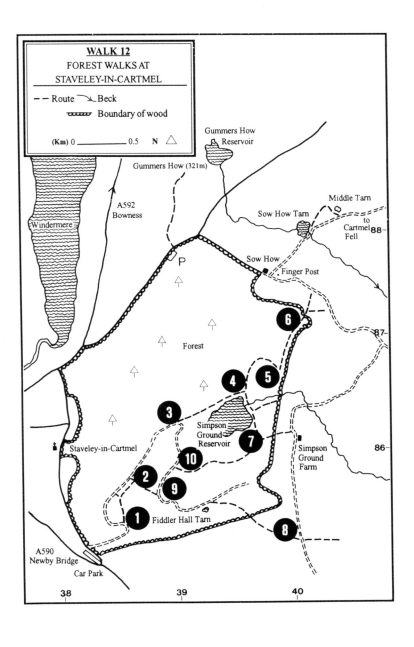

and in an adjacent section of disused road. There is waymarking within the forest.

From the entrance, proceed up the hill, following the dry forest road or the wet waymarked path (1) to rejoin the road at (2). Continue north-eastwards to the acute bend (3) where the waymarked path continues to the reservoir. At the dam (4), turn left to the forest's walled boundary (5) and left again to the stile (6). Cross the open ground to the unfenced road and continue leftwards along it to the fingerpost. Turn right to Sow How Tarn, then on to Middle Tarn just inside the walled woodland. Circle back to Sow How and return to the path junction (5) within the forest boundary. Continue south beside the boundary wall, crossing the outflow from the reservoir. The path curves south-westwards to the dam, turns south and divides (7). Here there is a choice: south-westwards, or right, to the forest road; or eastwards through the gate to Simpson Ground Farm and south along the bridle road to re-enter the forest by a footpath 1km (½ mile) further on by the path (8) – beware the bull! If the latter route is taken, Fiddler Hall Tarn will be seen on the left just beyond the point where the path joins the forest road. Some 300m (330yds) further on, a path branches left (9) to link with the outward route (2).

If you take the south-westerly path (from 7) you will join the forest road (10). Here you can turn left and walk 250m (275yds) to where the path branches right (9). At this point you have a choice between doubling back to Fiddler Hall Tarn or giving up and returning to the start.

Angling in Lakeland

The National Rivers Authority issues rod fishing licences valid in England and Wales. These run for one year and are obtainable locally in Lakeland from many fishing tackle shops and tourist information centres. A licence must be held by freshwater anglers, in addition to permits or tickets to fish specific waters. Children between the ages of 12 and 16, pensioners and registered disabled anglers receive concessionary rates; there is no charge for children under 12 years.

Anglers should be aware of bye-laws affecting fishing in their area, or on specific waters. In Lakeland two points should be underlined:

1 Lead weights are not completely banned, as some people believe. Weights *greater* than 28.35 g (1 oz) or *smaller* than 0.06 g (or up to no. 8 shot) may be used. The weight band between must *not* be used as this range has proved detrimental to swans and other wildlife.

2 Certain rare fish are protected. It is illegal to take: (a) Schelly (found in Ullswater, Brotherswater and Red Tarn); (b) Vendace (not found in any tarns, but present in some western lakes). Char, although classified as a rare fish, is not at present sufficiently endangered to be protected.

In addition to the rod licence, many tarns require fishing permits. Tarns listed in the index as inaccessible to the general public are obviously not available to the angler either. In some, fishing rights are restricted to members of an angling club only, but many of the high tarns offer free fishing.

Most anglers find lowland tarns more congenial than the high tarns, because they require less effort and time to get to, and yield larger fish. Consequently the pressure on such tarns necessitates some control in order to preserve fish stocks. The costs of restocking and maintenance have to be recouped from association membership fees and visitors' permits, so anglers who dip their rods without permission will be liable to prosecution.

The lists below suggest some tarns which may be of interest to the visiting angler.

The following abbreviations are used:

WADAA – Windermere, Ambleside and District Angling Association

AA – Angling Association

LTS – Local tackle shops.

Tarns Requiring Tickets or Permits

TARN	PAGE	TICKETS/PERMITS	FISH
Barngates Tarn	30	Drunken Duck Hotel, Hawkshead (Tel. 05394 36347)	Trout
Bigland Tarn ·Bigland Trout Fishery	173	Bigland Hall County Sporting Estates (Tel. 05395 31361)	Coarse Trout
Blea Tarn, Langdale	96	Tickets from Mrs Myers, Blea Tarn Farmhouse (just up the road from the tarn)	Trout and coarse
Blelham Tarn	30	Hawkshead Angling Club, Mr F. Hilton, Hawkshead Co-op, Main St, Hawkshead (Tel. 05394 36244)	Trout and coarse
Cleabarrow Tarn	47	Controlled by WADAA, permits from LTS or Smyths Records, Kendal (Tel. 0539 729595)	Trout and coarse
Cogra Moss	134	Contact Lothians Tackle Shop, Main St, Cockermouth (Tel. 0900 822006)	Trout
Dubbs Reservoir	45	Controlled by WADAA, permits from Ings Service Station (A591) or LTS	Trout
Ghyll Head Reservoir	54	Controlled by WADAA, permits from Beech Hill Hotel, Windermere (Tel. 05394 42137) or LTS	Trout

TARN	PAGE	TICKETS/PERMITS	FISH
High Arnside Tarn	31	Controlled by WADAA, permits from local Tourist Information Centres	Brown and rainbow trout (fly only)
Holehird	43	Contact members of the Lakeland Horticultural Society at the gardens (*not* the Cheshire Home or entrance lodge)	Coarse
Loughrigg Tarn	28	Contact Mrs Murphy, Tarn Foot Farm (Tel. 05394 32596), beside the tarn	Pike and perch
Moss Eccles Tarn	39	Controlled by WADAA, permits from The Tower Bank Arms, Near Sawrey, Hawkshead (Tel. 05394 36334)	Trout (fly only)
Ratherheath Tarn	50	Controlled by WADAA, permits from Plantation Filling Station (A591) and LTS	Coarse
School Knott Tarn	47	Controlled by WADAA, permits from the local Tourist Information Centre and LTS, Windermere	Trout (fly only)
Watendlath Tarn	147	Permits from Mrs Richardson, Fold Head Farm, Watendlath, Borrowdale (Tel. 07687 77255)	Trout
Whinfell Tarn	67	Tickets from Borrans Farm near the shore, information on fishing in Kendal area from Carison Fishing Tackle, 64 Kirkland, Kendal (Tel. 0539 724867)	Coarse fishery with perch, rudd, roach, tench, pike and eels
Yew Tree Tarn	34	Controlled by Coniston and Torver AA, tickets from Nicholson's Sporting Shop, Tilberthwaite Ave, Coniston (Tel. 05394 41639)	Trout

Tarns Where Fishing is Restricted

TARN	PAGE	OWNERS/MEMBERS	FISH
Devoke Water	83	Millom and District AA	Trout
Gurnal Dubs	62	Kent AA members only, Secretary, P. Bayliss, 9 Fountain Brow, Kendal	Brown and rainbow trout (fly only)
Hayeswater	121	Penrith AA	Trout and perch
Kentmere Tarn	59	Private fishing	Trout
Linthwaite House Hotel Tarn	52	Hotel guests only	Trout
Little Langdale Tarn	98	Private fishing	Trout, pike and perch
Mockerkin Tarn	133	Haig Angling Club, Whitehaven	Eels, pike and perch
Overwater	162	Private fishing	Trout
Podnet Moss	55	WADAA members only	Trout
Seathwaite Tarn	104	Furness Fishing Association	Trout
Tarn Hows	32	Private fishing	Pike, perch, roach and rudd

Tarns Which Offer Free Fishing

Small brown trout are known to reside in all these waters.

TARN	PAGE	TARN	PAGE
Alcock	25	Blea, Eskdale	77
Angle, Langdale	87	Blea water	124
Beacon	169	Bleaberry	136
Blea, Armboth	148	Blind, Coniston	102

TARN	PAGE	TARN	PAGE
Bowscale	164	Harrop	148
Burnmoor	75	Red, Helvellyn	115
Codale	95	Scoat	73
Easedale	94	Small Water	125
Goat's Water	102	Sprinkling	87
Grisedale	116		

For fishing at Angle Tarn, Patterdale, permission should be sought from the landowner at Beckstones Farm, Patterdale.

Waters Other Than Tarns

Although this book concentrates on tarns, anglers are interested in fish – be they in tarns, lakes, rivers or ponds – so I have taken the liberty of extending the coverage for their benefit. The following notes are not intended to be comprehensive and do not extend beyond the National Park boundaries. Again, local tackle shops and Tourist Information Centres will provide details.

LAKES	TICKETS/PERMITS	FISH
Brothers Water	Fishing is free on the eastern shore	Trout
Buttermere	Permits from Mr and Mrs Parker, Dalegarth, Buttermere (Tel. 07687 70233) or Lothians Tackle Shop, Cockermouth	Trout, char, pike and perch
Coniston	Some fishing is free except where notices state to the contrary; check at Nicholson's Sporting Shop, Coniston (Tel. 05394 41639) for local bye-laws and current regulations	Trout, char pike and perch

LAKES	TICKETS/PERMITS	FISH
Crummock Water	Apply to Rannerdale Farm, Buttermere (Tel. 07687 70232) or Lothians Tackle Shop, Cockermouth	Trout, char pike, perch and salmon; sea trout from July
Derwentwater	Controlled by Keswick AA, permits from Field and Stream, 79 Main Street, Keswick (Tel. 07687 74396)	Trout and coarse
Ennerdale Water	Contact W. N. Holmes, Main St, Egremont (Tel: 0946 820368 or 0946 820911), for weekly permits	Trout, pike perch and char
Esthwaite Water	Hawkshead Trout Farm, Fold Gate (Tel. 05394 36541), on western shore of the lake. A block NRA rod licence is held (£2 per week). Day permits are £9.25 in high season with reduced rates for pensioners and juniors. Boats available; open all year	Rainbow trout
Grasmere	Controlled by WADAA, tickets from Ambleside Tourist Information Centre (Tel. 05394 32582) or LTS	Pike, perch and eels
Loweswater	Apply to Waterend Farm, Loweswater (Tel. 0946 861465) or Lothians Tackle Shop, Cockermouth	Trout and coarse
Rydal	As for Grasmere	Pike, perch and eels
Ullswater	Free fishing	Trout, pike and perch
Wastwater	No fishing	
Windermere	Free fishing	Trout, char, perch and pike

RIVERS	TICKETS/PERMITS	FISH
R. Brathay	As for Grasmere	Pike and perch
R. Duddon	Members of Millom and District AA only; for membership information apply to Hools Tackle Shop, 185 Rawlinson St, Barrow-in-Furness (Tel. 0229 430425)	Brown trout, sea trout and salmon
R. Irt	Weekly permits from Gosforth Anglers Club, 11 Fell View, Gosforth, Seascale	Trout, salmon and sea trout
R. Rothay	As for Grasmere	Trout, perch and pike

Note

The above details were believed to be correct at the time of going to press, but circumstances alter and it's no good waving these pages under the nose of an irate water bailiff, keeper or landowner as proof of one's rights. It's up to the individual angler to ensure that the information given here is still accurate.

Bibliography

Fitter, R. and Fitter, A., *Collins Guide to the Grasses, Sedges, Rushes and Ferns of Britain and Northern Europe*, Collins, 1984

Griffin, A. H. *Inside the Real Lakeland*, Robert Hale, 1961

Jeffries, Michael and Mills, Derek, *Freshwater Ecology: Principles and Applications*, Belhaven Press, 1990

Heaton Cooper, W., *The Tarns of Lakeland*, The Heaton Cooper Studio, Grasmere, 1960

Holgate, J. and Parkinson, G., *Anglers Guide to the Lake District* (Castabout Series), Westmorland Gazette, 1987

Keble Martin, W. *The Concise British Flora in Colour*, Michael Joseph, 1971

Macan, T. T. and Worthington, E. B., *Life in Lakes and Rivers*, Collins, 1972

Marr, J. E. 'The Tarns of Lakeland' and 'Additional Notes on the Tarns of Lakeland', *Geological Society Quarterly*, 1895 and 1896

Smith, R. A., 'The Lakes And Tarns of Cumbria', *The Cumberland Geological Society, Proceedings, 1986–87*

Stokoe, Ralph, *Aquatic Macrophites in the Tarns and Lakes of Cumbria*, Freshwater Biological Association, 1983

West, Thomas, *Guide to the Lakes in Cumberland, Westmorland and Lancashire*, Richardson and Urquet, 1778

Wordsworth, William, *Guide to the Lakes*, Oxford University Press, 1835 (Paperback edition, 1977)

Further Reading

Cumberland Geological Society, *Lakeland Rocks and Landscape: A Field Guide*, Ellenbank Press, 1992

Fryer, Geoffrey, *A Natural History of the Lakes, Tarns and Streams of the English Lake District*, Freshwater Biological Association, 1991

Index and Checklist of Tarns

This alphabetical list of tarns can be used as an index to the main text and also as a checklist for tarn-hunters who wish to record the date on which each tarn has been visited.

In addition to page number and rough location, this list also indicates the relative difficulty of reaching each tarn, and whether or not it is accessible to the general public.

The following abbreviations are used for regions:

SE: South-East   SW: South-West
NE: North-East   NW: North-West
NO: Northern Outlying SO: Southern Outlying

The letters A, B, C, etc. refer to areas within each region, as designated in the main text. Thus, for example, 'SE–A' refers to South-East Region, Area A.

Each tarn is also graded from 1 (quite easy) to 4 (difficult), according to its distance from the nearest public road, the ruggedness of the terrain, and the level of route-finding ability required.

The grades have been allocated as follows:

1: Tarns which may be reached by clearly marked paths and are within 500m (550yds) of a public road.

2: Tarns less than 2km (1 mile) from a public road but where strong footwear may be required to tackle rugged paths.

3: Tarns more than 2km (1 mile) from a public road, or tarns where paths may be unclear or absent and some route-finding ability may be required.

4: Remote tarns requiring practical route-finding ability and hill-walking experience with regard to judging suitable weather conditions and being appropriately equipped.

Many tarns are situated within private grounds or on agricultural land. Those labelled 'Viewing only' can be viewed from nearby public paths but not approached; those labelled 'Accessible' are open to the general public; and those labelled 'Inaccessible' have no public access whatsoever.

TARN NAME	PAGE	AREA	GRADE	ACCESS	DATE VISITED
Alcock	25	SE–A	2	Accessible	———————
Angle (Lang.)	87	SW–D	4	Accessible	———————
Angle (Pat.)	122	NE–B	3	Accessible	———————
Arnsbarrow	108	SW–H	3	Accessible	———————
Atkinson	53	SE–H	1	Viewing only	———————
Barfield	85	SW–C	2	Viewing only	———————
Barngates	30	SE–B	1	Viewing only	———————
Baysbrown	27	SE–B	1	Viewing only	———————
Beacon	169	SO–A	2	Accessible	———————
Beckhead	145	NW–D	4	Accessible	———————
Bigland	173	SO–B	2	Accessible	*3-5-09*
Birk Haw	106	SW–H	2	Accessible	———————
Blackbeck	142	NW–D	3	Accessible	———————
Black Beck	172	SO–B	2	Viewing only	———————
Black Moss	67	SE–K	2	Viewing only	———————
Blea (Armboth)	148	NW–E	3	Accessible	———————
Blea (Esk.)	77	SW–B	3	Accessible	———————
Blea (Lang.)	96	SW–F	1	Accessible	*11-4-94*
Blea Water	124	NE–C	2	Accessible	———————
Bleaberry	136	NW–B	3	Accessible	———————
Blelham	30	SE–B	1	Accessible	———————
Blind (Con.)	102	SW–G	3	Accessible	———————
Blind (Esk.)	79	SW–B	3	Accessible	———————
Boltons	54	SE–H	2	Viewing only	———————
Boo	101	SW–G	2	Accessible	———————
Boretree	172	SO–B	2	Inaccessible	
Borrans Res.	45	SE–F	2	Inaccessible	
Borwick Fold	48	SE–G	1	Viewing only	*25-10-94*
Bowscale	164	NO–B	3	Accessible	———————
Brandreth	145	NW–D	3	Accessible	———————
Bright	166	NO–B	1	Viewing only	———————
Broadcrag	89	SW–D	4	Accessible	———————
Brown Cove	120	NE–A	3	Accessible	———————
Brownrigg	152	NW–E	3	Accessible	*30-10-99*
Brownstone	40	SE–E	2	Accessible	———————
Burney	170	SO–A	1	Viewing only	———————

TARN NAME	PAGE	AREA	GRADE	ACCESS	DATE VISITED
Burnmoor	75	SW–A	3	Accessible	_____
Canny Hill	173	SO–B	2	Accessible	_____
Carlside	163	NO–A	4	Accessible	_____
Caudale Head	57	SE–I	2	Accessible	_____
Caw Moss	106	SW–H	3	Accessible	_____
Cleabarrow	47	SE–G	1	Accessible	_____
Codale	95	SW–E	3	Accessible	_____
Cogra Moss	134	NW–A	2	Accessible	_____
Crook Res.	49	SE–G	2	Inaccessible	
Cunswick	56	SE–H	2	Viewing only	_____
Dalehead	139	NW–D	3	Accessible	_____
Devoke Water	83	SW–C	1	Accessible	_____
Dock	149	NW–E	3	Accessible	_____
Dockey	26	SE–A	2	Accessible	_____
Dubbs Res.	45	SE–F	2	Viewing only	_____
Easedale	94	SW–E	2	Accessible	_____
Eel	79	SW–B	2	Accessible	_____
Eskdale Green	77	SW–B	1	Inaccessible	
Fiddler Hall	178	SO–C	2	Accessible	_____
Flass	72	SW–A	1	Accessible	_____
Flat	67	SE–K	1	Viewing only	_____
Floutern	137	NW–C	3	Accessible	_____
Four Stones	127	NE–C	2	Accessible	_____
Foxes	90	SW–D	4	Accessible	_____
Galls	46	SE–F	1	Inaccessible	
Ghyll Head Fish Pond	54	SE–H	1	Viewing only	_____
Ghyll Head Res.	54	SE–H	1	Viewing only	_____
Ghyll Pool	63	SE–J	2	Accessible	_____
Goats Water	102	SW–G	3	Accessible	_____
Goosey Foot	36	SE–D	2	Accessible	_____
Grayrigg	68	SE–K	1	Viewing only	_____
Great Green Hows	171	SO–B	2	Inaccessible	
Greenburn Res	99	SW–F	3	Accessible	_____
Greendale	73	SW–A	3	Accessible	_____
Green Hows	171	SO–B	1	Viewing only	_____
Greenup Edge	151	NW–E	4	Accessible	_____
Greycrag	58	SE–J	4	Accessible	_____
Grey Knotts	144	NW–D	2	Accessible	_____
Grisedale	116	NE–A	2	Accessible	_____
Grizedale	37	SE–D	2	Accessible	_____

TARN NAME	PAGE	AREA	GRADE	ACCESS	DATE VISITED
Gummer's How	174	SO–C	2	Viewing only	_____
Gurnal Dubs	62	SE–J	2	Accessible	_____
Haber Tarn	129	NE–C	2	Inaccessible	
Hagg Pond	41	SE–E	2	Inaccessible	
Hard	118	NE–A	3	Accessible	_____
Harrop	148	NW–E	1	Accessible	_____
Haskew	129	NE–C	3	Accessible	_____
Hayeswater	121	NE–B	2	Accessible	_____
Haystacks	144	NW–D	3	Accessible	_____
Heights	177	SO–C	2	Inaccessible	
Helton	178	SO–C	1	Viewing only	_____
High Arnside	31	SE–C	2	Accessible	_____
High Dam	171	SO–B	2	Accessible	10-4-94
High House	91	SW–D	4	Accessible	_____
High Man	37	SE–D	2	Inaccessible	
High Moss	40	SE–E	2	Accessible	30-10-99
High Nook	134	NW–B	2	Accessible	_____
High Rigg (Tarns on)	155	NW–F	2	Accessible	_____
High Scawdel	141	NW–D	2	Accessible	_____
Hodsons	41	SE–E	2	Inaccessible	
Holehird	43	SE–F	1	Accessible	_____
Holehouse	83	SW–C	3	Accessible	_____
Holme Ground	35	SE–C	2	Accessible	_____
Holmes Head	29	SE–B	1	Accessible	_____
Innominate	143	NW–D	3	Accessible	_____
Jenny Dam	49	SE–G	1	Inaccessible	
Juniper	36	SE–D	1	Accessible	_____
Kelly Hall	107	SW–H	1	Accessible	_____
Kemp	61	SE–J	2	Viewing only	_____
Kentmere	59	SE–J	2	Accessible	_____
Kepple Cove	119	NE–A	3	Accessible	_____
Kirkfell	145	NW–D	4	Accessible	_____
Kittleton	170	SO–A	1	Accessible	_____
Knipe	53	SE–H	1	Viewing only	_____
Lambfoot Dubb	88	SW–D	4	Accessible	_____
Lang How(e)	94	SW–E	3	Accessible	_____
Lanty's	117	NE–A	2	Accessible	23-10-94
Latrigg	45	SE–F	1	Viewing only	_____
Launchy	141	NW–D	2	Accessible	_____
Launchy Gill	149	NW–E	3	Accessible	_____
Levers Water	103	SW–G	3	Accessible	_____
Lily	28	SE–B	2	Accessible	_____

TARN NAME	PAGE	AREA	GRADE	ACCESS	DATE VISITED
Lily Pond	40	SE–E	2	Accessible	
Lingmoor	97	SW–F	3	Accessible	
Linthwaite Ho. Hotel	52	SE–H	1	Inaccessible	
Little	161	NO–A	1	Viewing only	12-4-95
Little Langdale	98	SW–F	1	Viewing only	
Little Ludderburn	55	SE–H	1	Viewing only	
Littlewater	127	NE–C	1	Viewing only	
Lodge Head	37	SE–D	2	Inaccessible	
Long Moss	108	SW–H	1	Accessible	
Loughrigg	28	SE–B	1	Accessible	
Low Birker	81	SW–B	2	Accessible	
Low Eskholme	84	SW–C	2	Inaccessible	
Low	74	SW–A	3	Accessible	
Low Water	103	SW–G	3	Accessible	
Middle	176	SO–C	2	Accessible	
Middle Fairbank	48	SE–G	1	Viewing only	
Middlerigg	45	SE–F	1	Viewing only	
Mockerkin	133	NW–A	1	Viewing only	27-3-96
Mortimere	29	SE–B	1	Viewing only	
Moss Dub	138	NW–C	3	Accessible	
Moss Eccles	39	SE–E	2	Accessible	30-10.99
Moss Side	51	SE–G	1	Viewing only	
Muncaster	84	SW–C	2	Viewing only	
Out Dubs	43	SE–E	1	Viewing only	
Overwater	162	NO–A	1	Viewing only	12-4-95
Parkgate	76	SW–B	2	Accessible	
Peggy	68	SE–K	2	Viewing only	
Pewit	170	SO–A	1	Accessible	
Podnet Moss	55	SE–H	2	Accessible	
Potter	63	SE–J	2	Accessible	
Priest Pot	42	SE–E	1	Viewing only	
Ratherheath	50	SE–G	1	Accessible	
Red (Helv.)	115	NE–A	3	Accessible	
Red (Lang.)	99	SW–F	2	Accessible	
Red Crag	123	NE–C	4	Accessible	
Red Screes	57	SE–I	3	Accessible	
Robinsons	41	SE–E	2	Inaccessible	
Rose Castle	33	SE–C	1	Accessible	
Rough Hill	128	NE–C	1	Accessible	
Routen Beck (Low.)	65	SE–J	2	Inaccessible	

TARN NAME	PAGE	AREA	GRADE	ACCESS	DATE VISITED
Routen Beck (Up.)	64	SE–J	2	Inaccessible	
Rowanthwaite Pond	50	SE–G	1	Inaccessible	
Sawrey Stricely	38	SE–D	1	Inaccessible	
Scalebarrow	130	NE–C	2	Accessible	
Scale Head	40	SE–E	2	Accessible	30-10-99
Scales	164	NO–B	3	Accessible	
Scandale	56	SE–I	3	Accessible	
School Knott	47	SE–G	2	Accessible	
Scoat	73	SW–A	3	Accessible	
Scream Point	51	SE–G	1	Inaccessible	
Seathwaite	104	SW–G	3	Accessible	
Simpson Ground Res.	177	SO–C	3	Accessible	
Siney	78	SW–B	3	Accessible	
Skeggles Water	60	SE–J	3	Accessible	
Skelsmergh	65	SE–K	2	Viewing only	
Slew	29	SE–B	1	Inaccessible	
Small Water	125	NE–C	2	Accessible	11-4-94
Snipeshow	154	NW–F	1	Accessible	
Sow How	175	SO–C	2	Accessible	
Sprinkling	87	SW–D	4	Accessible	
Sprinkling Crag	87	SW–D	4	Accessible	
Steel Fell	152	NW–E	3	Accessible	
Stickle (Dun.)	110	SW–I	1	Accessible	
Stickle (Lang.)	92	SW–E	2	Accessible	
Sticks	119	NE–A	3	Accessible	
Stonehills	52	SE–H	1	Viewing only	
Stony	80	SW–B	3	Accessible	
Styhead	85	SW–D	4	Accessible	
Taggleshaw (High)	64	SE–J	2	Inaccessible	
Taggleshaw (Low)	64	SE–J	2	Viewing only	
Taggleshaw (Middle)	64	SE–J	2	Inaccessible	
Tarn at Leaves	153	NW–E	3	Accessible	
Tarn Hill (8 Tarns)	110	SW–I	2	Accessible	
Tarn Hows	32	SE–C	1	Accessible	25-10-93
Tenter Howe	61	SE–J	2	Accessible	

List of
Alternative Tarn Names